The Making of Pioneer Wisconsin

THE MAKING OF PIONEER WISCONSIN

Voices of Early Settlers

MICHAEL E. STEVENS

WISCONSIN HISTORICAL SOCIETY PRESS

Published by the Wisconsin Historical Society Press
Publishers since 1855

The Wisconsin Historical Society helps people connect to the past by collecting, preserving, and sharing stories. Founded in 1846, the Society is one of the nation's finest historical institutions.
Join the Wisconsin Historical Society: wisconsinhistory.org/membership

Excerpts from Harry H. Anderson, ed., *German-American Pioneers in Wisconsin and Michigan: The Frank-Kerler Letters, 1848-1864* (Milwaukee: Milwaukee County Historical Society, 1971), reprinted with permission of Milwaukee County Historical Society.

Excerpts from Theodore Christian Blegen, *Land of Their Choice: The Immigrants Write Home* (University of Minnesota Press, 1955), copyright © 1955 by the University of Minnesota, renewed 1983.

Excerpts from Gunnar J. Malmin, trans. and ed., *America in the Forties: The Letters of Ole Munch Ræder* (University of Minnesota Press, 1929), copyright © 1929 by the University of Minnesota, renewed 1957.

For permission to reuse material from *The Making of Pioneer Wisconsin: Voices of Early Settlers* (ISBN: 978-0-87020-889-8; e-book: 978-0-87020-890-4), please access www.copyright.com or contact the Copyright Clearance Center, Inc. (CCC), 222 Rosewood Drive, Danvers, MA 01923, 978-750-8400. CCC is a not-for-profit organization that provides licenses and registration for a variety of users.

The cover image, depicting a Wisconsin landscape in 1848, is one of fourteen agricultural murals commissioned for and originally displayed at the 1948 Wisconsin State Fair in celebration of the state's centennial. Donation and restoration of the murals was made possible through the generous financial support of the Kohler Foundation, Inc. The nine remaining murals are preserved in the Wisconsin Historical Society's permanent collections.

Photographs identified with WHI or WHS are from the Society's collections; address requests to reproduce these photos to the Visual Materials Archivist at the Wisconsin Historical Society, 816 State Street, Madison, WI 53706.

Printed in the United States of America
Designed by Ryan Scheife, Mayfly Design

22 21 20 19 18   1 2 3 4 5

Library of Congress Cataloging-in-Publication Data

Names: Stevens, Michael E., author.
Title: The making of pioneer Wisconsin : voices of early settlers / Michael
   E. Stevens.
Description: Madison, Wisconsin : Wisconsin Historical Society Press, [2018]
   | Includes bibliographical references and index. |
Identifiers: LCCN 2018013991 (print) | LCCN 2018021743 (ebook) | ISBN
   9780870208904 (EBook) | ISBN 9780870208898 (pbk. : alk. paper)
Subjects: LCSH: Frontier and pioneer life—Wisconsin. |
   Pioneers—Wisconsin—Biography. | Pioneers—Wisconsin—Sources. |
   Immigrants—Wisconsin—History—19th century. | Wisconsin—Emigration and
   immigration—History—19th century. | German
   Americans—Wisconsin—History—19th century—Sources.
Classification: LCC F584 (ebook) | LCC F584 .S74 2018 (print) | DDC
   977.5/03—dc23
LC record available at https://lccn.loc.gov/2018013991

For Elise, Hugo, and Lila-Rose

CONTENTS

INTRODUCTION

The Making of Pioneer Wisconsin tells the story of how a half million people uprooted themselves from familiar surroundings, traveled across vast distances, adapted to different environments, and created a new society. It is a process that has been repeated over millennia at different times and places. This story focuses on a generation of pioneer settlers who came to Wisconsin from the mid-1830s through the 1850s. In a twenty-five-year period, they helped grow Wisconsin's population from a little more than eleven thousand in 1836 to more than a half million in 1855 and more than three quarters of a million by 1860.

Rather than offering a traditional narrative, this book presents the stories of pioneer men, women, and even children in their own words. By reading their letters, diaries, and other writings, we become aware of their emotions and see the world through their eyes. The documents selected for this volume primarily focus on the ordinary stuff of life—moving to a new place, setting up a household, finding a spouse, making a living, keeping and discarding old customs, and contributing to a community. They offer vivid descriptions and the emotional reactions of a generation dealing with rapid change. What did it feel like to move to a new place that was being rapidly populated? How did settlers adapt to others who had different customs, traditions, languages, and ways of life? How did they experience weddings, childbirth, sickness, and depression in their new surroundings? How did they make a living in a new land? This mass migration included English-speakers from the eastern United States as well as Europeans who spoke a variety of languages. Despite their differences—and there were many—the early settlers of Wisconsin shared a common story of being uprooted, adapting, and building something new. Now, of course, we know how their stories turned out, but the future was uncertain for these settlers at the time of their writing, and they documented the process with both excitement and trepidation. Collectively, they provide us with the authentic voices of Wisconsin's pioneers.

The story is told in three chapters—bookended by a prologue and an epilogue—covering the settlers' migration, adaptation, and creation of communities. The prologue reminds us that pioneer settlements were built on losses borne by Wisconsin's Native peoples, who were subject to a federal policy that aimed to remove all Indian Americans west of the Mississippi River. In 1830, the Native population of Wisconsin outnumbered the non-Native population. But by 1850, the white population outnumbered the Native population by fifty to one. In a speech by Hoowanneka (or Little Elk) included in the prologue, the Ho-Chunk orator compares his tribe's interactions with the French, the English, and finally the Americans. He plaintively closes by asking American treaty negotiators, "Do you want our country?" For the Ho-Chunk, the unfortunate answer was yes.

Not only were the tribes physically displaced, but their separate, distinct cultures as Ho-Chunk or Ojibwe or Menominee soon became blended in settlers' minds under the single word "Indian" or "red man." Only a few of the pioneers represented in this volume actually met individual American Indians. Instead, they held in their mind an image of "the Indian," characterized by derogatory words such as "depraved," "uncivilized," or "wild" that could be used to contrast with the world they hoped to create.

The first chapter focuses on the experience of coming to Wisconsin after Indian land cession treaties had been signed and large numbers of American Indians had been removed. Many settlers described the desire to move as an itch, or a fever, impelling them to satisfy their curiosity and explore this new place. New Englander Henry Eggleston expressed it well, telling his wife, "I got thinking about Wisconsin and the more I thought about it, the more I wanted to see." Published and unpublished reports of newly available land circulating in the eastern states and in Europe inspired thoughts about Wisconsin. Christian Traugott Ficker, a German immigrant who settled in Mequon, even published a guidebook in his native country called *Friendly Adviser for All Who Would Emigrate to America and Particularly to Wisconsin*.

After settlers decided to move west, they experienced the journey—whether over land or by water—in different ways. Teenager Sarah Foote kept a diary of her family's trip west by wagon. Passing her Ohio schoolhouse provoked "the saddest of all leave-takings," but she soon found the trip exciting. On her arrival in Wisconsin she told her diary: "So now here we are all of us, ready to begin life in the woods." Charles Minton Baker, who came west from Vermont by wagon as well as by a Great Lakes ship, found the trip unpleasant. He commented on the incredible variety of humanity he encountered, "from almost every tongue & nation the rich & poor, the civil & uncivil, the neat & quiet, the noisy & dirty, the pious & praying, the impious & swearing, the genteel & fashionable & gay, & the ragged & filthy & disgusting." Noting the "crying & scolding & snoring & groaning," Baker said it was "a scene which I do not soon wish to experience again." Those who crossed the ocean often faced the greatest challenges. Ocean travelers described disputes between immigrants from different countries, bad food, and rough seas in which "none of us could remain on our feet." At the same time, some settlers were also moved by unexpected glimpses of whales and icebergs. Once on dry land, the travelers had to get to their destination in the West and find a way to make a living. One immigrant was pleased with the good wages he found in Mineral Point but lamented the gender imbalance, complaining about all the bachelors in his area. He told his friend in England, "You might bring a flock of lassies."

Once arrived, settlers went through a period of adaptation, which is the subject of the second chapter. The adjustments to climate, customs, and other challenges varied based on one's good or bad fortune, as well as one's temperament. One Norwegian settler explained that immigrants came to Wisconsin with "High hopes that we should be happy," and the most optimistic settlers viewed challenges as opportunities. A pioneer in Mineral Point tried to muster some enthusiasm while reporting that four inches of snow had already accumulated on the ground by the end of October. He wrote, "Nevertheless, our winters, though perhaps some-what colder, are much more pleasant and healthy" than the "half-cold, half-warm, wet, disagreeable, slushy weather" found back home. All the optimism in the world, however, could not protect those who lacked access to the services that they had been accustomed to in their former homes. Although health care in the nineteenth century was primitive compared to what we know today, one pioneer woman from New England living in the Lake Superior region lamented the loss of her child, writing, "Had there been a skillful physician at hand, in an unnatural birth, they might have saved our child. . . . My heart hungers for my babe."

Feelings of loneliness due to separation from family made life diffi-cult for many settlers. Racheline Wood Bass, on learning that her sister rejected her pleas to come west, wrote, "I have to-day had a little cry on the above account." Learning a new language also challenged immigrants from non-English-speaking countries. John Kerler Jr., a German immigrant, wrote, "Since English is spoken in court, trading, and in general (you find this all over North America) it is a little hard at first," although he pointed out that it was less of a problem in Milwaukee because of the large number of German speakers found there. Others wrote rhapsodically about their new home. George Adam Fromader was delighted with the rich bounty of food in Wisconsin compared to his diet in Germany: "Here in America one eats meat every day, sometimes twice—morning and evenings we have coffee." Experiences varied. For every immigrant who wrote "do not think of coming to America at all. . . . Do not let America enter your thoughts any more," there were others who wrote delightedly, "In this country everybody is free to do as he pleases as long as he remains orderly and respectable." Eventually, the sense of newness ended. As one immigrant put it, "One gets accustomed to everything by and by, and once the nut is cracked the kernel tastes better in the end."

The book's third chapter shows how settlers made new permanent homes for themselves and participated in creating or changing civic institutions. The chapter opens with accounts of people creating farms, homes, or families. Establishing a farm meant becoming accustomed to agricultural practices in North America; practicing a trade meant working according to the customs of the new land. One German immigrant offered this advice: "Do not imagine that when you step upon American soil the people will marvel at you, as such an extraordinary worker." A recent bride wrote to her new in-laws across the ocean, providing details about her wedding and setting up a household over her husband's store. Both foreign-born and American-born pioneers built new institutions, but the foreign-born had to decide which old ways should be retained and which should be discarded. One German-born Wisconsinite warned his former countrymen, "Be sensible; stop being a German and be an American." A Norwegian, worried about the declining use of the Norwegian language among young people, took a different approach, noting, "Their English is quite correct, but as soon as they start to speak their mother tongue, it generally sounds broad and clumsy."

American-born settlers, too, had worries about the loss of certain standards and regulations found in their home states. Many expressed anxiety about Wisconsin's disorderly and wild reputation. With frontier violence and shootings taking place, even in the territory's legislative chambers, people worried that news of such events might discourage future settlement. One observer noted unconventional behavior in a courtroom, where one of the attorneys "had a pitcher of Whiskey brought into the Court room, and set on the table before him, from which he drank long and frequently, so frequently that before he got half through with his speech he reeled to an fro, and staggered like a drunken man." To correct social problems, many settlers attempted to build institutions or change laws. Some sought to stop drinking and gambling through religion, organizations, or regulation. Others opposed these efforts, such as a group of men from Muskego who were worried that a proposed ban on beer sales would "multiply the water drinking classes of creation to such an awful extent." Others tried to reform race-based laws by advocating for a national ban on slavery, stopping enforcement of the fugitive slave law, or granting voting rights to black citizens. Both white and black Americans worked on these issues. Black settlers in Wisconsin, though few in number, were vocal on behalf of their rights. Joseph Barquet, a twenty-seven-year-old African American bricklayer, stated: "We are Americans by birth; the blush of shame comes to my cheek when I think of it, that the land of our nativity refuses us her protection."

Pioneers knew that they were living in a time of remarkable change. The book closes with an epilogue containing reflections written between 1838 and 1847 from settlers in Mineral Point, Racine, and Milwaukee. Even before statehood, settlers were awed by the changes that had taken place in their lifetimes and were aware of what one of them called the "Wisconsin Character." Hard work, self-reliance, and a public spirit characterized early Wisconsinites—at least in their own minds.

—‖—

During the half century from the end of the American Revolution to the mid-1830s, the land that would become Wisconsin was nominally under American control. It was governed, in theory, by a succession of territorial governments, starting with the Northwest Territory, followed by the Indiana, Illinois, and eventually Michigan Territories. Despite theoretical federal sovereignty, the land we now know as Wisconsin was contested for much of the half century after the end of the Revolution. The British maintained troops in the area until 1815. French Canadian traders, some of whom had intermarried with Native peoples, held a strong economic influence. During this time, American Indian tribes effectively controlled much of what became the state. With territorial government offices located hundreds of miles away, federal control was largely nonexistent.

All this began to change with the withdrawal of the British at the conclusion of the War of 1812. Rather than a three-way division of de facto control among the British, the French Canadians, and the Indian tribes, power now shifted toward the US government. Initially, small numbers of US troops were stationed at forts in Wisconsin, but a national policy that sought removal of the Native tribes in the West laid the groundwork for a massive influx of white settlers. A series of Indian treaties, most dramatically those starting in 1829 and continuing through the 1830s, opened much of Wisconsin to in-migration. Despite the cession of land by the tribes, not all of the state's indigenous population was willing to move or stay west of the Mississippi River. The Ho-Chunk (Winnebago), the Menominee, and the Ojibwe (Chippewa) continue to maintain a substantial presence in Wisconsin to this very day. In addition, members of tribes in New York—the Oneida, Stockbridge, and Brothertown Indians—moved to Wisconsin as a result of pressures to move Indian Americans increasingly farther west. Yet, the state's Native population was drastically reduced by the middle of the century. An 1825 estimate cited by the land speculator James Duane Doty suggests that Wisconsin's American Indian population that year was 25,000. By 1850, the population was reduced to 6,500.

In 1834, government offices opened and began selling land that had been acquired from American Indians by treaty, which set off a rush of settlers to Wisconsin. In April 1836, Congress passed a law establishing the Wisconsin Territory. Over the following twenty-five years the non-Native population grew rapidly, as seen in the following table.

By 1850, nearly all non-Indian adults in Wisconsin had been born outside of the state. About 43 percent of the residents had

WISCONSIN NON-NATIVE POPULATION[1]	
1836	11,683
1840	30,945
1846	155,277
1847	210,546
1850	305,390
1855	522,109
1860	775,881

been born in the United States but outside Wisconsin. The greatest number of these came from New York and New England, and most were white— only 635 black people (about two-tenths of 1 percent) lived in the state that year. About another 35 percent of the state's residents were foreign born. The majority of these (about 55 percent of the foreign born) were non-English-speaking immigrants who had come from the German states, Scandinavia, Switzerland, and the Netherlands, with the Germans being the largest group. About 45 percent of the immigrants spoke English, and most of these had come from the British Isles. The remainder of the state's total population—the roughly 63,000 who were born in Wisconsin—were largely the young children of settlers.

When Wisconsin became a territory in 1836, the largest settlements were in the southwest, where nearly half of the territory's population lived and where a mining boom was taking place. That was soon to change. By 1840, when the territory's population had tripled to more than 30,000, the population growth occurred in the southeastern part of the territory in what are now Milwaukee, Racine, and Walworth Counties in the southeast. Ten years later, the state's population had grown tenfold to more than 300,000 and nearly a quarter of its residents lived along the Lake Michigan coast. Most of those who came to Wisconsin were farmers, although the growing numbers created opportunities for skilled and professional work- ers who lived in urban areas. By 1850, nearly one in ten Wisconsinites lived in an urban area, and that ratio grew to one in seven by 1860. Milwaukee was the state's fastest-growing city, increasing in population from 1,712 in 1840 to 20,061 in 1855. Also contributing to this growth was the fact that later settlers were more likely to arrive in traditional family units. In 1840, Wisconsin had eight males for every five females. By 1850, the ratio had been reduced to six males for every five females.

In less than a quarter century, Wisconsin acquired a very different look and feel. A person who left Wisconsin when it became a territory in 1836 and returned in 1860 would have been astounded by the changes that had taken place. The sheer number of new people, the variety of languages, the construction of cities, and the growth of social, political, and religious institutions would have shocked the observer. The men and women who settled Wisconsin were well aware of these changes as they occurred, and their words that appear in this volume convey that recognition. Their voices express anticipation, excitement, inspiration, and disorientation at living in a new world, one partially of their own making.

—||—

With two exceptions, all of the historical documents included here were written between 1833 and 1854, with three quarters written prior to statehood in 1848. The writers came to Wisconsin by boat, train, or wagon. The American-born settlers largely came from New England, New York, Ohio, and Kentucky. Most of them were white, but those represented in this volume include an American Indian woman from the Brothertown tribe, as well as African Americans—some of whom had been formerly enslaved and some born free. The European immigrants whose documents appear here came from Germany, England, Norway, Holland, and Switzerland. One letter writer was born in Wisconsin of mixed European and Native ancestry.

The pioneers whose writings are represented here lived in various parts of Wisconsin but were largely from the areas of heaviest settlement, namely southeast of a line drawn from Prairie du Chien to Green Bay. From the eastern part of Wisconsin, authors include those who settled in or wrote from modern Brown, Kenosha, Manitowoc, Milwaukee, Ozaukee, Racine, Walworth, Washington, and Winnebago Counties. The southwest, which was the earliest part of the state to be settled, is represented by writings from Grant, Green, and Iowa Counties. In the north, we hear from pioneers in modern Ashland, Juneau, and Pierce Counties.

Only a fraction of early settlers left written records, and many of these are routine financial or government documents. Any existing collection of this sort was shaped by those who were literate and has survived thanks to families who saved the writings, as well as luck and chance. Materials were chosen for this book based on quality of description, emotional feeling expressed, and experiences described. The texts come from a variety of sources, with citations provided in the endnotes. Some are from manuscripts of letters and diaries that were saved and deposited into archives and libraries. In other cases, the originals have been lost but transcripts were made more than a century ago and deposited in archival institutions or were published. In an era before news wire services, letters home were often shared and published in newspapers for the larger community to read. Still other documents were written for publication by immigrants attempting to encourage others in their homeland to come to Wisconsin.

While many of the documents found here were written in English, others are accessible to an English-reading audience because they had been previously translated and subsequently published. As a result, documents originally written in German, Norwegian, or Dutch often read more smoothly in English because the spelling and grammar reflect the proficiency of the translator rather than that of the original writer. English-language texts taken from original manuscripts and contemporary newspapers are transcribed literally, with spelling and grammar corrections noted in brackets when needed for clarity. In documents taken from later publications or transcripts, obvious errors made by the printer, translator, or scribe have been silently corrected. Clarifications and corrections inserted by this editor are always noted in brackets. Words that are underlined in the original are rendered here in italics. Omitted parts of the text are noted with ellipsis points. Formatting and spacing in the original have not been reproduced. Any exceptions to these editorial practices are noted in the headnote to the document.

—||—

This book had its genesis during the 1990s when I was working as State Historian of Wisconsin at the Wisconsin Historical Society. At that time, I was editing a series entitled *Voices of the Wisconsin Past,* which includes five volumes outlining different aspects of the state's history in the words of those who lived through the events. This book was originally intended to be part of that series. My appointment as State Historic Preservation Officer in 2004 put this project to a halt, leaving a substantially complete manuscript. My retirement from the Society in 2013 allowed me to return to it with new perspectives on immigration, settlement, and community building. I reworked the manuscript, eliminated some writings, added some additional documents, rewrote my commentaries on the documents, and wrote new introductory material.

What appears here is truly the result of the work of many hands. Archivists, historians, and translators who collected, preserved, and published materials—many of whom did their work in the nineteenth and early twentieth centuries—ensured that the record of pioneer Wisconsin would be available to readers of the twenty-first century. The process of researching, gathering, selecting, editing, and organizing the material would have been impossible if not for the work of talented research assistants during the 1990s. Most of these were graduate students at the University of Wisconsin–Madison, many of whom have gone on to distinguished careers. These research assistants did prodigious survey work of early Wisconsin material, locating documents that appear in this and earlier volumes. Steven Burg and Sean Adams found much of the material contained here. Sean made additional contributions to the manuscript with his research, preparation of draft notes, and valuable ideas. Charmaine Harbort's transcription of documents was critical. Ellen Goldlust-Gingrich copyedited an earlier version of the manuscript, and proofreading by Ellen and Sean helped ensure the text's accuracy. During the last year, John Kaminski and Jonathan Reid at the University of Wisconsin–Madison offered help in deciphering some particularly challenging text.

At the Wisconsin Historical Society Press, I thank Kathy Borkowski, who was the Press's director when the manuscript was submitted and accepted for publication. Her leadership and vision helped create a first-rate publishing operation. Kate Thompson, then–editor in chief, promptly responded to my proposal with enthusiasm and helped ensure that the book moved forward. Liz Wyckoff, my editor at the Press, improved this manuscript in innumerable ways, especially with her careful (and artful) improvement of my prose. Having worked in publishing myself, I know there are many other hands that helped turn this manuscript into a book, who remain anonymous to even me. Thank you to the entire team—from editorial to production to marketing—whose good work makes working with the Press such a pleasure.

Therese Stevens provided a critical eye on various drafts of the manuscript, assisted with the proofreading, and served as a sounding board for ideas. Her greatest contribution is her constant love and support. This book is dedicated to my three grandchildren, Elise, Hugo, and Lila-Rose, who will find their own way to pioneer in the twenty-first century.

Prologue

"Do you want our country?"

Cultures in Conflict

The creation of the new federal territory of Wisconsin in 1836 and the signing of Indian treaties during the previous decade opened a new part of the West to white settlement. Prior to that time, the land we now know as Wisconsin was the site of military and cultural conflicts among the various peoples who sought to make a home there. During the previous two centuries, Europeans had explored, traded goods, and fought in the land that lay between Lake Michigan and the Mississippi River. Still, French, British, and American settlements during these years were haphazard, and they only minimally challenged the American Indians for whom Wisconsin was home. As long as the French and British (and later the British and Americans) fought over control of North America, Wisconsin's American Indian population could play one party off the other. But with the victory of the United States in the War of 1812 and its consolidation of control over the old Northwest, the American Indian peoples of Wisconsin lost much of their strategic importance. The land that became known as Wisconsin would no longer be a sparsely populated area marked by a contest of cultures. In fact, it soon became a destination for a rapidly growing American population, operating under the belief that settlement of the entire continent was part of its destiny.

Hoowanneka (or Little Elk), a Ho-Chunk orator, offered his summary of Wisconsin's past and expressed concern over its future in a

HOO-WAN-NE-KA,

A WINNEBAGO CHIEF

Lithograph of Hoowanneka (or Little Elk), Ho-Chunk, 1842, from Thomas L. McKenney and James Hall's *History of the Indian Tribes of North America*, Vol. II. WHI IMAGE ID 91336

speech at Prairie du Chien, recorded by Caleb Atwater (1778–1867) in July 1829. An Ohio lawyer, politician, and writer, Atwater had been appointed in 1829 as one of three federal commissioners to negotiate the American acquisition of the rich mineral country south of the Wisconsin River and east of the Mississippi—land that was, at the time, Ho-Chunk territory. Hoowanneka's impassioned words offer an interpretation of Wisconsin's past that not only demonstrates an understanding of the cultural differences between French traders, English "Red Coats," and American "Blue Coats," but also offers a haunting challenge to federal Indian policy.

The first white man we knew, was a Frenchman—he lived among us, as we did, he painted himself, he smoked his pipe with us, sung and danced with us, and married one of our squaws, but he wanted to buy no land of us! The "Red coat" came next, he gave us fine coats, knives and guns and traps, blankets and jewels; he seated our chiefs and warriors at his table, with himself; fixed epaulets on their shoulders, put commissions in their pockets, and suspended medals on their breasts, but never asked us to sell our country to him! Next came the "Blue coat," and no sooner had he seen a small portion of our country, than he wished to see a map of THE WHOLE of it; and, having seen it, he wished us to sell it ALL to him. Gov. Cass, [i.e.,Lewis Cass, governor of Michigan Territory, which included Wisconsin] last year, at Green Bay, urged us to sell ALL our country to him, and now, you fathers, repeat the request. Why do you wish to add our small country to yours, already so large? When I went to Washington, to see our great father [President John Quincy Adams], I saw great houses all along the road, and Washington and Baltimore, Philadelphia and New York are great and splendid cities. So large and beautiful was the President's house, the carpets, the tables, the mirrors, the chairs, and every article in it, were so beautiful, that when I entered it, I thought I was in heaven, and the old man there, I thought was the Great Spirit; until he had shaken us by the hand, and kissed our squaws, I found him to be like yourselves, nothing but a man! You ask us to sell all our country, and wander off into the boundless regions of the West. We do not own that country, and the deer, the elk, the beaver, the buffalo and the otter now there, belong not to us, and we have no right to kill them. Our wives and our childr[e]n now seated behind us, are dear to us, and so is our country, where rest in peace the bones of our ancestors. Fathers! pity a people, few in number, who are poor and helpless. Do you want our country? your's is larger than our's. Do you want our wigwams? you live in palaces. Do you want our horses? your's are larger and better than our's. Do you want our women? your's now sitting behind you, (pointing to Mrs. Rolette [Jane Fisher Rolette, wife of fur trader Joseph Rolette] and her beautiful daughters, and the ladies belonging to the officers of the Garrison,) are handsomer and dressed better than our's. Look at them, yonder! Why, Fathers, what can be your motive?[2]

The answer to Hoowanneka's question—do you want our country—was clear. The following month, the Ho-Chunk signed a treaty that ceded land in southwestern Wisconsin to the federal government. This was only one of a series of treaties signed by Wisconsin tribes that were designed to open the territory to white settlement. Between 1829 and 1833, all land rights south of the Fox–Wisconsin waterway had been acquired by the federal government. Over the next two decades, the Ojibwe, Potawatomi, Menominee, and other tribes gave up additional land. By 1848, nearly all of the new state of Wisconsin was no longer in Indian possession. While federal policy envisioned removal of the entire tribal population of Wisconsin west of the Mississippi River, Indian peoples survived, either through treaties establishing reservation land or by the return of some tribal members who had been removed to the west. Nonetheless, over the quarter century between 1825 and 1850, the American Indian population of Wisconsin would decline from 25,000 to 6,500 while the white population increased from 3,000 to more than 305,000.

1

"I GOT THINKING ABOUT WISCONSIN"

Journeying West

In November 1834, the federal government started selling public land in Wisconsin at $1.25 an acre, setting off a great rush of settlers to the territory. Americans looking for better prospects moved west, and Europeans seeking to improve their lives in a new country crossed the ocean. Over the next quarter century, Wisconsin's white population grew from about 11,000 to more than 750,000. Visitors to Wisconsin stoked this fire by publishing glowing accounts of the prospects for early settlers. L. H. Nicholls of Lockport, New York, penned one example of this enthusiastic booster-style journalism. In addition to describing the climate, land, and laws of the territory, Nicholls even told his readers the best ways to travel west. His letter originally appeared in the October 1840 issue of *The New Genesee Farmer and Gardener's Journal* of Rochester, New York, and was later reprinted in a Wisconsin newspaper from which the text below is taken.

Lockport, [New York]

Sept. 19, 1840

Messrs. Editors.—Having recently visited the Territory of Wisconsin, and examined it with reference to its agricultural importance, I have thought perhaps a hasty sketch of its soil and climate, and its general inducements to emigrants, might interest the readers of your journal. Wisconsin lies on the west side of Lake Michigan, and is bounded west by the Mississippi river, containing an area of land considerably larger than the State of

New York. It is at present divided into thirteen counties, only the southern portion of it being surveyed and organized into thirteen counties. It now contains a population of about 31,000 inhabitants, having increased over 12,000 within the last two years. The climate is more temperate than the same latitude in the State of New York; there is more fair weather, and less rain and snow, than in New York; from what cause I know not, but the thermometer and the metereological table kept in the Territory, prove this to be so. Experienced agriculturalists residing [in] the Territory, say the seasons are longer there than in the State of New York, and I am inclined to think it is true, as vegetation was two or three weeks in advance of us when I was there. Wisconsin is a rolling country, in some places hilly, though not too much so. There are scarcely any swamps in it unless it be in the north part and west of the Wisconsin river. The rivers, creeks, and small lakes, which are numerous, contain clear water generally supplied from the springs with gravelly bottoms—consequently the inhabitants are not subject to the ague and fever or any bilious complaints. On the whole, I am of opinion that Wisconsin possesses a milder and as healthy a climate as that of New York.

The country generally, with the exception of the Lake shore, consists of prairie and bur-oak openings, and the soil is equal probably to any in the world. It consists of a deep sandy loam, easy of cultivation, and produces large crops of wheat, corn, and all the coarser grains; the rate of production equals that of the best land in Western New York. There is probably not timber enough in some parts of the Territory to supply the wants of the agriculturalists, but this can in a great measure be remedied by planting locust and other forest trees, which grow with great rapidity. The chief inducements to emigrants are the cheapness of lands, healthy climate, and the facilities with which the farmer can commence operations. Land can be purchased second handed, for from $1.50 to $3.00 dollars per acre; or at Government price, $1.25 per acre. Farmers usually contrive to take part prairie and part openings. It costs now $2.50 per acre to break up prairie the first time, and after that one team will plough with ease. The openings are free from underbrush, and the farmers generally girdle the trees, and plough and sow among them without chopping. In this way they get good crops, the trees are about as wide apart as the trees in a common orchard. A farmer arriving in Wisconsin with $500, is about as well off as

BY THE PRESIDENT OF THE UNITED STATES.

IN pursuance of law, I, **MARTIN VAN BUREN,** President of the United States of America, do hereby declare and make known, that a public sale will be held at Green Bay, in the Territory of Wisconsin, on Monday, the fourth day of June next, for the disposal of the public lands within the limits of the undermentioned townships and fractional townships, to wit:

North of the base line, and east of the meridian.

Townships fifteen and sixteen, of range thirteen.
Township thirteen, of range fifteen.
Townships twelve, fourteen, and sixteen, and fractional township eighteen, of range sixteen.
Township thirteen, and fractional townships sixteen and seventeen, of range seventeen.
Fractional township twenty-seven, of range twenty-six.

Lands appropriated by law for the use of schools, military, or other purposes, will be excluded from sale.
The sale will be kept open for two weeks, (unless the lands are sooner disposed of,) and no longer; and no private entries of land in the townships so offered will be admitted until after the expiration of the two weeks.
Given under my hand, at the City of Washington, this fifth day of January, Anno Domini 1838.

M. VAN BUREN.

By the President:
JAMES WHITCOMB,
Commissioner of the General Land Office.

Broadside announcing sale of public land in Wisconsin Territory, 1838. WHI IMAGE ID 137169 a farmer here owning a farm worth $3000. Yet I would advise a man who is well enough off where he is, to stay there and let well enough alone. But a man who has a large family which he wishes to bring up as farmers, or a man who has but little to begin life with, had better emigrate to Wisconsin. I would rather have $100 in money in Wisconsin now to start farming with, than $500 here; the Wisconsin farmer will be the best off in five years. Wisconsin too, has fine openings for mechanics of almost every trade. Its laws are similar to those of this State, with few exceptions. The laws in favor of debtors are rather more liberal: $100 value of the farming utensils of a farmer, are exempt from execution, and they exempt many articles of furniture which are liable to be taken in this State. There is no imprisonment for debt arising upon contract; the laws in that respect being nearly a transcript from our statutes.

A farmer wishing to emigrate to Wisconsin, would take a steamboat, brig, or schooner, as the case might be, at Buffalo, and land either at Millwaukee, Racine, or Southport [Kenosha], and then go out into the country. Steamboats are usually about five days in going round, and sail-craft a few days longer; or emigrants may go by land, in which case they would go through Michigan to Chicago, and then strike into the Territory at any place they might wish. Sail-craft are much the cheapest, and are said to be as pleasant and quite as safe as steamboats. I suppose a family of five or six persons could go round in a brig and be found for $30 or $40. In conclusion, I will reiterate, that if a man is well off, stay where he is; if not, and he is willing to undergo some privations incident in all new countries, pack up and go to Wisconsin, particularly if he is a farmer or a mechanic.

Yours very truly,

L. H. Nicholls[3]

The opening of this new area also drew international attention as prospective settlers from a host of European nations considered the move to Wisconsin. Hundreds of guidebooks for potential immigrants were published in the first half of the nineteenth century, and European newspapers and bookstores included the same kind of boosterish accounts of Wisconsin as were found in American cities. One German who answered this call was Christian Traugott Ficker, who moved to the small farming community of Mequon, north of

Milwaukee, in the late 1840s. In response to inquiries from friends still in Germany, Ficker wrote a small book called *Friendly Adviser for All Who Would Emigrate to America and Particularly to Wisconsin*, which was published in German at Leipzig in 1853. In this excerpt from an English translation, Ficker responds to the question that many in Europe contemplated: who should immigrate to America?

Difficult and uncertain as it is to give any advice herein, I still undertake to answer this inquiry in the very simple manner following: (1) All who have the desire, the strength, and the endurance to take care of themselves in any situation, and who will not be ashamed to accept any kind of labor when necessary, even though unaccustomed to it; (2) All who in Germany live under political or religious oppression and desire to free themselves therefrom. If I were to go into particulars concerning the first class, I understand this to include very specially peasants and handicraftsmen, although among the latter (as I shall show later) not every one can count on procuring a good living immediately.

The land owner (farmer) if he can bring along so much money as to be able to buy at once an improved farm, and if such farm is large enough so that he can employ a hired man, he may live in a very happy and independent manner. Just as independent and fortunate, certainly, is the man who owns a smaller farm and can keep no hired man, but he must carry on his work personally. In this way, however, he usually manages to maintain a very good table. The reader should remind himself of what I have said in a former chapter about farming, that it is carried on here in a manner very much less systematic and at the same time, up to now, it brings in less cash than in Germany. Let no one imagine that he can mount his horse and set his numerous laborers to work here as he can in the Old Fatherland. That would be very expensive here since laborers in this country receive a very high wage. He who in Germany perhaps has many debts on his land and has to work very hard merely to keep the interest paid up, is probably best off here; as also he who has many (and among them some well grown) children who can be of great help in the beginning.

Laborers in America (on farms) are exactly like members of the family and are treated no differently either at table or otherwise. Women servants never work in the field here (or at least very rarely), but take care of the house, the kitchen, and at most the stable. Field work is exclusively the business of the men. Since the wages of these laborers is very high, they usually work only a few years and then they buy land for themselves and carry on their own farming operations. Here, however, I must warn everyone who wishes to serve in America that he should not allow himself to be betrayed by high wages to go into far southern regions. Thousands, and among them particularly new immigrants, have paid for this mistake with their health and even with their lives, since it was too hot and unhealthy for them. Once accustomed to the American climate, one can risk this better and even then he has to be very foresighted (particularly in the use of fruits).

Among the handicraftsmen who can count upon prompt support here are particularly the tailors, who receive excellent wages in the towns; the shoemakers, especially if they have already learned in Germany not to sew the soles, but (as is always done here) to nail them with wooden pegs; the smiths, the wagonmakers, the coopers, the cabinetmakers, the carpenters, the millwrights (as also in general all workers in wood), the butchers, the stonemasons, the brewers, the hat makers, the locksmiths and gunstock makers; lacemakers and stocking workers if they settle in a city; the millers if they have money enough to buy or build themselves a mill; the saddlers, the brickmakers, etc.

Among the handicraftsmen who might find it more difficult to secure situations I count the bakers, who only occasionally find work in the cities, since farmers in the country almost universally bake their own bread; the glaziers because here window frames are constructed in large factories and the windowpanes of appropriate sizes can be purchased in the stores and set in easily by the owner; the watchmakers if they do not have sufficient means to establish themselves at once as jewelers; the needlemakers because here needle ware is prepared in large factories or imported very cheaply; the barbers because that business in the cities is usually carried on by colored persons who are at the same time hair dressers; the bookbinders unless they are so fortunate as to make a connection with a large book business; the tinsmiths because tinware is now at least sold in prominent hardware stores; the horn turners because here tobacco is mostly smoked out of small clay pipes and German pipes are not at all the fashion; the dyers unless they can find employment with large manufacturing

This German advertisement for passage from Bremen to New York appeared in European newspapers. WHI IMAGE ID 137171

establishments of the East; the nailsmiths because here almost without exception machine-made nails are used; the ropemakers because the hemp and flax production is carried on very little so far.

Merchants do a good business here only they must be able to speak the English language. It is to be remarked (1) that here there is much barter for farm products so that generally the merchant has a double function, and (2) that generally, in smaller cities and in the country, a store has to be provided with everything that is needed. Here one finds fabrics, cut rope, glass, stoneware, iron, shoes, soap, drinks, tobacco and cigars, in short everything that buyers need. To fix prices and sell as this is generally done in Germany is not satisfactory to the American.

Horticulturists do a good business in or near a city because early products such as beautiful flowers are paid for at a very high rate. Last summer I was with a horticulturist in Milwaukee with whom I am very friendly. A gentleman had just sent his servant to him to bring several bouquets and plants. My friend had me write the bill since I was right there. It called for $17.50. In Germany I could not have given away the whole lot.

Lawyers, unless they are prepared to take in hand a four-to-five-pound axe, had better remain in Germany. In America the wheat is not yet sowed for them; since the administration of justice fortunately is much simpler here, and the men who dispense justice possess sufficient sound, human understanding they do not always consider the rigid law but also talk of justice.

Musicians, particularly good piano teachers, if they are unusually good, find excellent support in the larger cities. But I advise everyone to bring along the necessary instruments and strings since these are exceedingly expensive here. In the country knowledge of music provides incidental income for the musical farmer, but he cannot live from it.

Doctors and surgeons if they are skilled in their profession are well paid both in the city and in the country.[4]

The decision to relocate far away from family and friends was no easy one for most early settlers. However, the anticipation of such a strenuous journey did not keep settlers with "Wisconsin Fever" away from the region.

Henry Seymour Eggleston (1820–1862) was struck with "Wisconsin Fever" on the way to work in the summer of 1849. Eggleston was originally from Vermont and, after marrying Elizabeth Washburn, lived in Potsdam, New York. However, Eggleston soon began to hear about opportunities in Wisconsin from members of his family and friends from Potsdam who had moved there. After a brief stay in Michigan, Eggleston moved to Wisconsin and sent for his wife and young daughter, Mary, to join him. The Egglestons later lived in Appleton, where Eggleston became postmaster, and in Ripon. In this early letter to his wife, Henry Eggleston shows that although the journey west was a demanding one, the presence of familiar faces in this new land helped to soften his adjustment to Wisconsin. His letter also includes an early use of the word "Badger" to refer to a resident of the state.

Richmond Walworth Co Wisconsin
Friday Aug. 17. 1849

Dear Elizabeth,

You see I am at last in the midst of the *Prairies,* and although I have never yet been out of sight of land, I have been twice out of sight of timber, and they tell me I have seen nothing yet that looks like a Prairie, so I suppose there is something a little nicer ahead. When I wrote you last from Marshall I told you to direct your next letter to me at that place, thinking I should stop there, till a letter would get back to me, but I got thinking about Wisconsin and the more I thought about it, the more I wanted to see it, and a week ago last Saturday, after Breakfast, I made up my mind to start the next Monday, and started off for the R Road to go to work but before I got to the Shop, I made up my mind that I could not wait till Monday so when I got to the Shop I told the Boss I wanted to settle, and at 1 Oclock P.M. I was in the Cars bound for the promised land. I got into New Buffalo at 6 Oclock, 109 miles, Fare from Marshall $3.30 we had to stop here over night, as there was no Boat leaving for Chicago till the next morning. At 6 Oclock we started on board the Steamer *Pacific* for Southport, touching at Michigan City, Chicago, & Little Fort, and arrived at Southport at 4 P.M. (Sunday) Fare across $3.00, Monday morning I started in the stage for Salem 16 miles. Fare 75 cts. Got to Carolines at 10 A.M. found Uncle Daniel & Aunt Clara there, they were all well except Caroline who is quite unwell, but you will probably have an opportunity of judging for yourself by the time you receive this, as she starts with her folks for N York next Monday. She thinks of stopping there about a year. Robinson wanted to let his place to Madison & me but I did not dare to take it for I was afraid Madison would not want to stop so far East. The next day after I got there he commenced thrashing. His Wheat like others in this vicinity is a good deal injured by the rust especially *Winter* Wheat. I staid with them untill the next Monday when I took the Stage and started off in pursuit of William's. I went as far as Geneva 16 miles and here I found I wanted to turn North through Elkhorn & from there to Sugar Creek, as Richmond is the next town west of that. From Geneva across, there is no Stage. but I found a young fellow going to Elkhorn, and got a ride with him. Staid there over night and the next morning hired the Landlord to carry me to Wm's (10 miles). As they keep a Grocery I thought I would play *possum* a little and see if they remembered me. So I marched into the House leaving my trunk in the Wagon, and as soon as I got into the door I enquired of Harriet (as there was no one else in the House) if she had any Beer, she told me she had. Says I lets have a couple of glasses, but she did'nt make any move toward the Beer barrel, but stood right in her tracks looking me in the face for a minute or more, before she could make out who I was, and then she begun to laugh and says she "Seymour Eggleston you can't come it. I guess I know you yet" so I did'nt have any chance for speculation there. I found them all well & hearty. William was at work on a School House, which he is building by the job, about 100 rods from his House, he boards at home. Ellen, Josephine & Seth had grown so that I should not have known them, if I had seen them any where else. They have got a little "Badger" here that they call *Martha Elizabeth*, probably you wont remember her, as she must have been very small, when they left Potsdam. She is smart as a Whip. The country right about Williams is "Openings" and rather uneven. "Rock Prairie," lies about 4 miles West and "Sugar Creek" Prairie about 1 ½ miles East. I think I should not pick out William's farm if I was calculating to get my living by farming altogether, on account of its being somewhat broken by what they call "Bluffs." Uncle Daniel will tell you what they are. His land with this exception is first-rate soil, and bears great crops. His Wheat that he raised this year is plump handsome Wheat as you ever saw. He has got as good a place for a Tavern, I believe, as there is on the road. This is the dullest season of the year, as the Farmers generally have not Thrashed, but there is more travel passing here now in One Day than there is on the Potsdam & Ogdensburgh road, in 3 Days certain & I guess more. The Lead from Galena is all taken through on this road which makes an immense amount of teaming of itself. I thought when I left Carolines, I should go on North, after stopping here a few days, but have pretty much concluded to stop & Work with William till you come. You will want to land at Milwaukie and you will find hundreds of teams, every day coming out from there, that have been in with Wheat so that you can get your luggage brought out pretty cheap and if you want to go through to Beloit. Stage fare is just the same from Milwaukie as from Southport $3.00. I should think it would be best to stow most of the Baggage at Milwaukie untill we look around & decide where we are agoing to stop & then we can send for it any day, by teams going in with Wheat. A man has just come in, who says that the *"Empire State"* on the 9th Inst. sprung a leak near the *Manitou Island* and sunk in 9 feet water. If this report should prove true, the Card I sent you by Uncle Daniel will be of no use. There was no lives lost. I have heard some great stories about the northern part of the State in the region of the Indian Reserve & Winnebago Lake. I am aching to see it, but believe I will wait till you come & we will take a tramp together. The government land is mostly taken up, about here, so that the chances for buying in this vicinity are rather scarce although there is plenty of second hand farms for sale, cheap say from 4 to 10 dollars per acre, with some considerable improvements. but I rather think we shall conclude to go North, where we can have a little better chance for choosing a location at government price [i.e., $1.25 per acre]. however we will decide that when we have seen for our selves. . . . I shall not try to tell you anything about the Country as Uncle Daniel can tell you more about it in 10 minutes than I could write in 10 hours so I will leave that part for him. And now about moving. Uncle Daniel will be able to tell you whether there is any danger *now* in coming through, and if there is, I of course would be the last one to urge you to come, but on the contrary would advise you to stay. but if they, after going through, should conclude that the danger from Cholera was past, and you should be ready for a start, I can assure you I should be tickled within an inch of my life to see your faces once more, and the quicker the sooner as the boy said. Your last letter I have not received yet but shall expect it now every day as I told the P.M. at Marshall to send it on as soon as it came into the Office. Be careful of little Mary on the road that there is no accident happens. And you must all be careful about being out much in the evening air. I had forgotten to tell you that I am as hearty as ever. Give my love to all of our folks & tell them to write to me often. I should have written before, but have been waiting for your letter, but I concluded not to wait any longer—Goodbye

H. S. Eggleston[5]

While there were many reasons that enticed men and women westward, the physical distance represented a significant barrier for prospective settlers from both eastern America and abroad. For example, in 1830 it took a solitary traveler from three to four weeks to travel from New York City to Wisconsin over a complicated route of turnpikes, canals, and rivers. Considering that most settlers came as families and often carried all their worldly possessions with them, the length and difficulty of this trip could prove to be substantial obstacles.

The following excerpts from Sarah Foote's (1829–1912) account of her family's trip by wagon from Ohio to Wisconsin illustrate the challenges of their month-long journey. When the Foote family decided to move westward to the Wisconsin Territory in 1846, Sarah resolved to keep a written journal of the journey. Although she was only a teenager with a country school education, Sarah's entries paint a vivid picture of her family's trek from Wellington, Ohio, to the town of Nepeuskun along the shore of Rush Lake in Winnebago County. Within a year of her arrival in Wisconsin, Sarah married William C. Smith. Her enthusiasm coupled with her sharp attention to detail recreates what must have been a common experience for many nineteenth-century pioneers in Wisconsin.

April 14, 1846. Tuesday evening and 'tis to be the last night for us here in our old home in Ohio, for all of our things are packed and all but what we most need were sent on by water to Milwaukee. The rest of the things nearly fill a large wagon.

Father, mother, Mary, Sarah, Orlena, Alvin and Lucy are to ride in the family buggy.

Tonight we girls are to stay with our schoolmates, Elvira and Samantha Bradley. Their brother Charlie is going with us to Wisconsin Territory to drive one of the teams. . . .

Apr. 15, 1846. Wednesday morning and pleasant. Many of our friends and neighbors gathered to see us off and after the usual exchanges of good wishes, goodbyes, and sad farewells we were on our way at 10 o'clock. As we passed the old school house it was the saddest of all leave-takings though a silent one.—

But we were soon away from home scenes and with many new objects gaining our attention our minds turned from sad thoughts to new and pleasanter ones. . . .

Sat. Apr. 18. We paid 75 cts. for our fare and all of us felt rather down, for we had had poor water to drink for a day or two, so different from what we were used to. Soon after starting today we came to two roads both leading to the same place, the right hand road leading through Cottonwood swamp and the left lead through a worse road so some had told us. Others declared the left hand road was better. Finally after a great deal of inquiry we took the right hand road.

We reached Michigan state line at noon, and stopped to rest and lunch. In three miles farther on we came to the great swamp and of all the roads we had seen this was the worst. The mud was deep and stiff except places where logs were laid across and this made it very rough.

We all walked most of the time, for it was so hard for the horses we had to stop and rest them very often.

It was only five miles but we were nearly all the afternoon getting through. They are commencing a turnpike through them and I hope it will be finished when we go back. After getting two miles out of the swamp we found better roads.

We put up for over Sunday at a new tavern and found it quite thickly settled about here. We travelled 20 miles today and feel tired and quite like resting. We find better water here and all are feeling better than in the morning. . . .

Tues. April 21. We slept uncommonly well for we were in nobody's way. We had for breakfast pork, potatoes, tea and sugar, and bread. After eating and washing the dishes, while Mother was placing things in order, we girls rambled about the place to find amusement, and all waiting for Father to return. We found plenty of sassafras growing and dug some roots for tea.

About 10 o'clock Father came back. He had gone on 9 miles the night before to find a wagon shop where he left the broken wheel and then came back a mile to a public house to stay over night. His bill for himself and team was one dollar. In the morning he borrowed a wagon wheel and came back to us and we were soon on our way to the village where we got our wheel fixed. We had to wait over an hour for Father to get the wheel which cost 18 shillings for being mended.

We finally got started in the afternoon and soon found better roads and country. We now began to see large fields of wheat growing and beautiful oak openings. These latter looked like large orchards to us. The trees are smaller with spreading branches, so different from the heavy timbers we have been used to seeing. We bo't two bushels of oats for 50 cts. We are now stopping for the night at a Temperance house which we have not usually found. This is also a very good place. . . .

Mon. Apr. 27. . . . Soon after leaving this place we came to very thick heavy timber where we found some wintergreen berries which were all new to us. We picked a good many by the road as we travelled. We finally came to a tavern that was built under a very large pine tree, and we stopped here to eat our dinner. After resting an hour we went on and found the roads very sandy.

We also found plenty of wintergreen berries and had plenty of time to pick them to, for the sand was so deep that the horses could not go out of a walk.

At about 4 o'clock we came to another fork in the road and as usual we took the right hand road. But of all the dismal places we had ever seen this was the worst. A thick forest was on one side of the road and on the other were great sandbanks nearly as high as the trees. And to crown all the (I thought) dismal roar of Lake Michigan could be heard in the distance beyond the sand hills. The roads where so bad we had to put part of the load from the wagon on to our buggy. Soon after we had done this we met a man who told us we would soon come to a road turning off from this road. But of all the crooks and turns this certainly beat all. The sandbanks grew higher and the distant though unseen roar of the lake grew louder.

We thought that if we were only on top of the highest bank we might see the great lake, a sight we had long wished for. So while the horses were resting Mary, Orlena, Alvin and Charles took a notion to climb the hills for a view. Mary and Orlena climbed the first hill but no lake was to be seen, only higher hills beyond met their gaze, so they turned back. But Alvin and Charles kept on yet they got only a far distant and faint view of the lake after all.

After the lake searchers came back we started on through the sand. We had been told at the last house we passed, that it was nine miles to the next tavern and we thought we could easily get through. But soon after this we were overtaken by a man in a buggy and he seemed to know all about the roads. He said it was only three miles to the next public house, and said we had such a heavy load we'd better let some of us ride with him, but we thought not! So off he went and we kept on and on. It grew dark and still no house was in sight. We were sure we had gone the three miles and more, so Father left us to rest or go slowly and went on alone to find a house. but he finally came back without finding any thing but the same sand hills, and so we concluded to camp out, for it was past 7 o'clock. We made a fire and found some water which we boiled in our iron tea-kettle. For supper we had some bread, butter, tea, and sugar. After supper we fixed a bed in the wagon for the boys and one in the buggy for the rest of us, all but Father. He rested in the forward part of the buggy and did not sleep much. . . .

Sunday May 3rd. This afternoon mother and cousin Bradley went with us girls to see the lake, and a pretty lake it is, so clear and still with its white pebbled banks sloping to the water's edge. We gathered a few white shells, and pretty stones. In returning we went through the village burying ground, a sweet retired place midst a grove of small trees. Cousin B— pointed out to us several graves covered by beautiful flowers, placed there by affection's hand. We enjoyed our walk very much and returned just as the sun was hiding behind the hills. It was to me a new and charming sight. It was a beautiful sunset on the wide and open prairie. I can not describe it nor can I ever forget the sweet thoughts that came into my mind. No words can express them and I'll not try. . . .

Friday May 8. . . . We have been through very pretty country all day. We all think that if it is as good land as this where uncle John and Henry are we shall be contented. At night we found no signs of a public house so enquired at a log house of a man who said he could keep us. So we took his word for it and stopped. But when we went into the place we found a hard looking situation. But as they said it was some ways to the next house we concluded to make the best of it and stay here.

Sat. May 9th. . . . After going a short distance away from the Settlement we came to a small stream over which was a bridge made of planks laid lengthwise and all loose. We thought it looked as though lumber was pretty scarce there. Mother thought we had better not ride across. but Father said, "Sit still all of you. I'll get out and drive very slowly and we shall get over all safe." We went on and got over except the back wheels of the buggy. They dropped down through between the planks, up to the hubs. Then Father said, "Sit still, I'll lift you out," and he did, so that we were finally over safe, for all our fright. About a mile farther on we passed a log shanty and three miles more another building, and then all was woods, prairie and oak openings. We finally came to a road leading off to the right. Father was much puzzled by this, but concluded after considerable hesitation to keep on this road. We went on until about dusk and then the bushes became very thick. It soon got so dark we could hardly distinguish any track but we kept moving slowly. Now and then we had to stop to look for the best crossing to a creek, and found the very best bad enough. It was not wide but deep. Father did not like to wait for us to all get out so with one or two exceptions we staied in the buggy. Many times we had hard work to keep from being thrown out, as the horses liked the plan of jumping across creeks rather than walking. We girls began to get very uneasy and began teasing Mother to know whether she didn't think Father was really lost and whether she thought we should ever find any body off here in this wilderness. But she told us to keep still and that all would be right, she guessed; and guessing was all that could be done I guess at that time. There was no moon but the night was clear so it was not very dark.

At last we came to a sort of turnout track and we stopped to investigate. After looking about we came across an upright stake or pole, split at the top and in this split was a stick crosswise. But owing to the darkness and our ignorance of that sort of guideboards, the affair was no guide to us so we kept on in the same track. We had not gone far before we got into trouble again by coming to a watery slough or marsh. The water got deeper and deeper and finally Father thought best to stop and call three times which he did. There we waited with anxious suspense and there came from a distance an answer, faint but from some person. We waited with great anxiety for several minutes and then heard some one or something coming towards us and right through the water too. Then when near enough the call came again and we all knew it was Uncle John!

After much rejoicing and glad explanations he told us that we must turn around and go back to the place where we saw that split stick, that they put it there as a guide to us to turn out. When we reached this place we went on and soon met Henry who had gone that way to find us, supposing we had taken this road. The road we started on they travelled in the winter when it was frozen and this one we were now on they used when the marsh was full of water. We soon found the way around the marsh and a jolly rejoicing crowd we were and when we reached the log shanty as they called it we were a happy company. There was Brother Henry, Uncle John and his wife Aunt Laura and little Harriet, and all so glad to see us!

We were now at our journey's end. We ate supper, and after talking for I don't know how long, we fixed beds on the floor of the shanty for most of us. and the boys slept in the wagon out doors, but we slept well.

Sun. May 10, 1846. . . . So now here we are all of us, ready to begin life in the woods, and here I must stop for the present, though I might continue and perhaps make it interesting too, but do not feel really capable; so here is an end to this journal for now.[6]

Yankees figured prominently in the early settling of Wisconsin. The sandy and stony soil of New England and the growing population of New York created pressures for many farmers, who often saw the new territory of Wisconsin as an attractive alternative. Using the water route opened up by New York's Erie Canal, settlers from this region poured into Wisconsin during the 1830s and 1840s. By 1850, the small state of Vermont had sent more than ten thousand people to the new territory, and in that same year the census revealed that a quarter of Wisconsin's settlers had come from New York.

Charles Minton Baker (1804–1872), a native of New York who grew up in Vermont, helped shape Wisconsin's society and institutions in its formative years. An attorney and businessman by profession, Baker settled at Lake Geneva in 1838 and became the first lawyer to practice in Walworth County. Baker quickly assumed a leadership role in his new surroundings and contributed to the legal and constitutional development of Wisconsin. He served as a member of the territorial council, a delegate to the Constitutional Convention of 1846, and a commissioner to revise the state's statutes in 1848 and 1849. Much to his chagrin, Baker traveled along with less distinguished settlers when he initially moved west with his wife, Martha, and three young children, Mary, Charles, and Edward. Baker's frustration contrasts well with the more light-hearted attitude of Sarah Foote.

Sept. 10, 1838, Left Hortonville [Vermont] loaded with the kindness of friends & neighbours & amidst their regrets & good wishes for Wisconsin. Arrived at Whitehall [New York], that rocky, muddy, dirty, crooked, contracted, outlandish outlet of creation, tucked in between marshes & mountains,—the abomination of all travellers & my especial abhorrence. Made arrangements for the shipment of my goods to Buffalo. Met with sundry little annoyances & vexations. . . .

Sept. 13. Stopped for the night at a Dutch tavern in Manheim on the Mohawk. Sheets & pillows so dirty that Mrs. B. would not sleep on them. Called at a Dutch tavern in the morning & the landlord a true Hollander "vondered vy we vent so far for." In afternoon called at another Dutch inn & could get nothing but sour milk altho' it was milked in the morning & it has been a cool day. Have passed thro' Mayfield, Johnstown, Palatine, St. Johnsville, (late Oppenheim) & Meridan into Manheim. Rained last night but was rather an advantage than a hindrance as it laid the dust. Country good & even excellent most of the way. Day rather fine & ride pleasant. . . .

Sept. 22 . . . We arrived at Buffalo at about 4 P.M. & drove directly thro' Main St. to the wharf having travelled today 34 miles. We were immediately beset with Steam Boat agents & in a short time engaged a passage on Board the Steam Boat *Bunker Hill* for Detroit. Being about the first on board we secured pretty good quarters. She is a large staunch built Boat with good Accommodations. She is to go out this evening or tomorrow morning. Buffalo is a flourishing place & doing an extensive business. She is destined to be a great place as the main outlet of the extensive & increasing trade of the upper lakes. Here is the starting point for the mighty West & from this point imagination stretches her wing over the great waters which reach nearly 2000 miles into the interior & roll their billows along the most fertile shores on the Globe. Hail thou fair & fertile West, thou world of floods & forests of bright rivers & green prairies, thou art henceforth my home. Great & magnificent West almost untouched & fresh as at thy first creation formed on a mighty scale & destined by thy Creator for events mighty as thyself. Great West the pilgrims & the poor man's home, thou invitest to thy bosom to partake of thy riches & thy bounty all alike of every rank of every clime & tongue. Onward be thy way & glorious be thy destiny. . . .

[September] 23 & 24 . . . It is very tedious lying in port especially as we are thronged & our numbers are continually increasing from almost every tongue & nation the rich & poor, the civil & uncivil, the neat & quiet, the noisy & dirty, the pious & praying, the impious & swearing, the genteel & fashionable & gay, & the ragged & filthy & disgusting. Found all my goods which arrived today & shipped them on board the brig Neptune for Milwauky at $6 per hundred. . . .

Sept. 26 . . . From Huron we directed our course to Cunningham's island which brought our boat into the troughfs of the sea when we had vomiting enough. Not Esculapius [the Greek god of medicine] & all his tribe could have produced so sudden & astonishing effect. Suffice it to say we had plenty of reeling & staggering to & fro & a most filthy & disgusting scene ensued in all parts of the boat. There were many pale faces among the fair & some awfully wry faces among the men. Some hung over the sides of the vessel & some lay stretched on chairs & settees & on the deck & floors in all manner of shapes & positions, whilst others were reeling & staggering wherever a lurch of the boat happened to throw them. It was curious to observe & contrast the glee & laughter of some few reckless characters who were unaffected with the solemn woe begone countenances of those who were sick. Mrs. B. & Mary were very sick, Charley was much affected & I had some very unpleasant sensations. We were thus exposed to rolling of the waves about 2 hours when we run under Cunningham's island to wood which completely sheltered us from the waves & the wind. This is a small island containing about 3000 acres is very fertile & settled by about 80 inhabitants. After lying to about 1 ½ hours we are again on our way direct to Detroit. The boat rides tolerably well.

[September] 27 . . . The scene presented in the deck cabin among the deck passengers is worthy the pencil of Hogarth [i.e., William Hogarth, an eighteenth-century British artist known for satirical illustrations]. Shades of night & my great grandmother. Here lie stretched in wild disorder & promiscuous confusion upon the floor like the slain on the field of battle in all shapes & positions both sexes & all ages, the man of gray hairs & the tender infant, the rosy cheeked damsel & the sturdy wood chopper. Here is crying & scolding & snoring & groaning. Some in births & some on chairs & trunks & settees & the rest on the floor. Some sitting & some lying, some dressed & some undressed, some covered & some uncovered & naked; some are stretched on beds, others on matrasses & cushions & cloaks & not a few are trying to find the soft side of the hard floor. Such is a steamboat life on lake Erie, a scene which I do not soon wish to experience again.[7]

Nineteen-year-old George Smith (1823–1879) moved from Ohio to Southport (now Kenosha) with his parents in 1843. Smith later rose to prominence in state politics, serving as state attorney general, the mayor of Madison, and a member of the state legislature. In this amusing account written to his friend James Sargent, Smith reveals how the genuine dangers of the journey could easily become magnified in the imaginations of fearful settlers.

Chicago
March 24th, 1843

Dear J.

. . . I will not attempt to give you a detailed history of our daily life on the way, or any kind of a description of the country or villages through which we have passed. The weather has been so cold & some of the time so blustering, that I have not paid much attention to the country. I have looked only to the road & I assure you it has oftentimes required some care to keep that. We passed through Michigan and one corner of Indiana, & I cannot tell how the country would look in its summer garments, but I assure you it looks uncomfortable enough in its winter robes—but I do not intend to describe to you the country—indeed for the reasons I have stated—my description would be but poor if I tried.

I will however give you a slight idea of the people & a few miles of the country through Indiana. I do this because here for certain reasons I noticed the country & scrutenised the people with more minuteness than elsewhere on my route. The section of Indiana through which we passed is regard[ed] in some respects a dangerous route. I mean that portion of it say 40 miles the other side of Michigan City. This city is about 40 miles from Chicago.

Somewhere in the neighborhood alluded to lives the notorious Bill Lathy formerly of Lathys corners, in Summit Co. & he is supposed to be the head & captain of a gang of horse thieves & counterfeiters—& hereabouts they live. We were warned to be on our guard in passing through this country. We had 6 very fine horses & some valuables besides—which under existing circumstances we could not well afford to loose. We tried to pass this infested district in one day, but the roads were so heavy from the depth of snow that night overtook us midway the distance, & we were forced to stop at what we had been told was a kind of headquarters for the scamps thereabouts. This was a low rakish dirty looking building, with a rickety sign in front on which was lettered, "Tavern." We drove up to the door, & out came Mr. Landlord. I wish you could have seen him—with his red bushy hair—his big bloated face & this by bad whiskey—which abounds in this neighborhood, & which is commonly called "red eye," literally dripping from his eyes—which were "red eyes" in truth. He was indifferently dressed yet fantastically, he had on a bright red vest much worn, a pair of green & red striped pantaloons and a big dirty green beige [word illegible] tied by the ends in front, & right at his heels were two big bull dogs that looked fierce & ugly enough—but not so bad as their master.

He said we could stay—he "sposed" whereupon we commenced to unload ourselves, & the little portable traps that we took in with us nightly when we stopped. We hardly commenced this unloading process when out came 5 or 6 of "Mine Hosts" croneys. I will not undertake to describe these characters to you. I will say however, that they reminded me of as many big black snakes, in a kind of half torpid state. Each man looked his part well. Of course we took them to be horse thieves, & our fears were excited that they might have been promoted to the higher degrees of crime for they certainly looked as if they were ripe for "treason stratagem & murder."

We would have gladly left this place, but stay we must. We determined therefore to pass a sleepless night in that house, & we did. At first they would have placed us in rooms distant from each other, but we declined this arrangement & succeeded in getting two rooms adjoining—Father & Mother & Charles & Lafayette occupied one room & Parsons & I another.

Our room looked out to the barn. We each had a big hickory cane & a Pistol; we watched the barn & listened intently all the night long in constant fear that some evil was to befall us. Once or twice during the night we thought we heard some unusual stir in the house & about the barn—but the morning and a bright beautiful cold morning it was—found us as safe from harm as if we had been lodged in a Princely Palace—save that we were wearied from watching. Our horses were all safe & they had been well cared for. A comfortable breakfast was prepared for us and about 9 A.M. we left the place where our fears had been so excited & I must say that all of the inmates of the house looked better to us than they did the night before. I have thought of the matter since, & I must do those rough fellows the justice to say that in estimating them we rather reasoned from our fears—they were rough looking men to be sure & what we heard excited our fears & we looked at these men with a distorted vision—at all events they did not molest us & in the morning they all seemed kind & obliging & the landlord assisted us with a will & a grace that would have done honor to "Mine Host" of a more elegant establishment.

We left them there thankful at least that our horses had not been stolen & that we had been permitted to depart in peace.[8]

Although the overland journey to Wisconsin could be a lengthy and difficult affair, the voyage from Europe taken by another brand of Wisconsin settlers was even longer and, in some cases, deadly. These European settlers looked to Wisconsin as a shelter from many different storms: religious persecution, political turmoil, economic hardship, and overcrowded conditions. But no matter the reason, for large numbers of German, Norwegian, Dutch, Swiss, Irish, and other European settlers coming to Wisconsin, one experience was common to all—the overseas journey. The crossing of the Atlantic Ocean, which usually took between one and two months, was far and away the most dangerous and uncomfortable portion of a family's passage to their new home in Wisconsin. The following accounts from German, Dutch, and Swiss immigrants reveal the incredible hardships that characterized these journeys, as well as the travelers' underlying sense of hope.

Gerhard Kremers (d. 1909) emigrated with his family from the Rhine Valley in Germany to Newton Township in Manitowoc County.

In this letter, originally written in German, Kremers claims to "have told the naked truth and have depicted the shadows as well as the sunshine" of the long journey to Wisconsin.

Manitowoc-Rapids, in the State of Wisconsin

July 26, 1848

... Following the painful day of separations, we took the train the next morning at Duisburg which brought us to Bremen the same evening. After a lapse of three days we went to Bremerhaven, where the anchors were weighed on the 19th of April. With good cheer and favorable wind we sailed down the ever widening Weser into the North sea. A truly great spectacle: the unbounded expanse of the sea makes an unforgettable impression on the admirer. However, the very next morning the sight had lost its sublimity for many. With a strong wind, which enabled us to make four [knots] per hour, the disagreeable seasickness made its appearance. Though by no means dangerous, it is accompanied by a sense of annoyance. Since this sickness has been described so often, it would be superfluous to describe it in detail though I could write from experience. Children are not affected, also some grown ups, among them my father. Favored by a strong wind, we entered the channel on the 3rd day and could see the cliffs of the English coast, however, for a short time only. A few days later we had to entrust ourselves to the waves of the Atlantic Ocean, which were readily recognized by their size. The wind became less strong and for 8–10 days we made little progress. But now there came a change. Suddenly toward evening a wind arose. It became stronger and stronger and bulged the sails. Waves 25 feet high crowded each other while their spray was carried away by the wind and struck with hissing sounds. Our small ship, which had only 130 passengers on board, tilted to the side so that occasionally the railing was on a level with the surface of the water. However, it made great progress (in an hour 6.) Trunks, tin containers, and other objects fell over. The dreadfulness was increased by the darkness of the night and the phosphorescence of the sea. The whole was of such a nature, that, as the sailors told us, we might get a fair idea of a storm, but that it could not be called such. Toward morning it became more quiet. Even in worse storms the voyage on the open sea is not dangerous though it is so near the coast. Anyone who desires to emigrate will not be induced to give up his plans

A Sunday on the High Seas during my crossing to America by Franz Hölzlhuber. WHI IMAGE
ID 28043

because of such contingencies. Moreover, accidents are very rare. Should
there be sufficient cause, we should not hesitate to entrust ourselves to
the waves again.—Our captain decided to avoid the gulf stream. We arrived on the grand bank of New Foundland. From here our course was in
a southwesterly direction, however, very slowly, along the American coast
as far as Long Island. This we first saw to our right with the mainland in
the distance. What a pleasant sight!—

Before proceeding, I shall say something about our provisions on board
ship. Our food was very poor: poor coffee, poor pork, and malodorous
beef; in addition we received bread, butter, peas, beans, barley, and rice.
Even these would not have been edible because of poor preparation had not
hunger spiced the meals. Several modest requests for a better preparation
of the food were rejected in a harsh voice. This incivility we could bear so
long as our own provisions lasted. These exhausted, our patience had an
end. Several of our traveling companions informed the captain in all seri-
ousness that he had to provide better food. This decisive demand produced
results. Whether angry or frightened, I know not, but the captain changed
color several times. From now on we, the passengers, prepared our own

food. So far as the material, delivered in sufficient quantity, was concerned it was good, the dishes prepared therefrom were palatable. However, such supplies as were poor to begin with could not be improved. Owner, captain, and cook all three were to blame. Others who sailed via Bremen had like experiences. We know full well, for we have been so informed by those who have had the experience, that boarding at one's own expense has its disadvantages, we are nevertheless of the opinion that others who desire to follow will do better to sail from Antwerp, Rotterdam, Havre, or London since by so doing they can board themselves. For families with children under twelve years of age it will also be cheaper, hence advisable.

But now let us return to the American coast which we approached very closely after we had taken on board a pilot. Every one was jubilant over our early arrival in the country which our eyes had sought so eagerly and so often. While Long Island spread out to our right, we could see the endless main land to our south. However, as we came closer, all was hidden by a dense fog. Night overtook us and the ship dropped its anchor. As the fog disappeared the next morning, we saw land close by. Words fail to describe how happy we were. It was as though winter had suddenly been replaced by spring. A beautiful panorama delighted the eye. On both sides beautiful knolls covered with a variety of trees and studded with country homes. At the foot of the hills white houses, one more beautiful than the other. Of interest also are the fortresses with their cannons. Before us and to our rear hundreds of masts of ships from all parts of the world. In addition, steamships, very different from the German ones, cross the bay. Here at quarantine, an hour this side of New York, every one was happy over the fortunate termination of our trip. Every one, feeling that to God alone belonged praise, gladly joined in singing 'Nun danket alle Gott' ["Now Thank We All Our God"] as proposed. Such a choral, sung on such an occasion, is uplifting. After a rapid and none too strict inspection of our baggage, and after the physician had done his duty, toward noon of the 37th day we were conveyed by a steamer to New York. An endless forest of masts of sailing vessels and of smoke stacks of the largest steamers stretches along the shore line of the city. Presumably but few cities afford a like sight. The impression made upon us was great. . . .

Gerhard Kremers
Son of Pet. Kremers formerly of Vluyn near Moers[9]

John Remeeus, a Dutch immigrant who came to America from the province of Zeeland in 1854, settled in Milwaukee with his wife and five children. Remeeus kept a diary during his voyage, and from the excerpts presented here, which appear in English rather than the original Dutch, one can sense not only the excitement and difficulties that accompanied his crossing of the Atlantic, but also the ways that ethnic conflicts were often reduced and moral standards were enforced while en route.

There were in Antwerp 2,700 emigrants, mostly Germans, waiting for ships to take them to America. For four weeks the winds had been blowing out of the wrong quarter; hence no ships had entered the harbors of Holland, Belgium, or Germany.

After we had enjoyed some food every man had to help bring the trunks, boxes, and other baggage on board. We were given permission to furnish our sleeping quarters as suitably as we wished. The women, in company of Messrs. Westven and Snoep, and of Vermeulen, the agent of the line, went to see the sights of the town. I was kept busy all afternoon fixing up my berth. I used a coarse wallpaper for this purpose. I also put up curtains around the bed and did everything I could to make our quarters pleasing and comfortable for my family. The captain and helmsman observed me while thus engaged and smiled kindly, thereby showing that they were pleased with what I was doing.

When I had finished this task, I went to the hotel to get mother and the children. This was the first night we slept in the ship that was to bring us to America. It was the bark "Fedes Koo" from Portland, Maine, commanded by Captain H. Higgens.

The next morning, June 1, we were busy bringing aboard provisions for our long voyage. Later, when this labor was finished, our names were called from a list, and two men distributed the food according to the size of each family. Provisions consisted of green peas, navy beans, rice, flour, ham, salt, and a small quantity of coffee and sugar. Everything was measured or weighed and had to be signed for. We were to receive potatoes and ship biscuit each week. We also were given enough bread to last about five days. . . .

June 9. Ditto. This day a baby was born to German parents. As soon as this became known, the captain and the helmsman made the necessary arrangements to help them and assigned special quarters to them. Considering the limitations of our space, the room soon was made as comfortable as possible; but it was not, of course, a proper room in which a Dutch mother usually delivers her baby. The child was born without the aid of a doctor. Our Dutch women on board were surprised at the manner the baby was taken care of. In Holland such things received far more elaborate attention. All this gave our Dutch women a great deal to talk about.

June 10. During the day calm weather, but toward evening the wind started to blow.

June 11. Today, the hardest wind we had as yet experienced. Many were sick, and mother who had been feeling so much better for the past few days was compelled to go to bed. The ship rolled violently.

We now learned what a terrific force water exerts when stirred by a gale. The ship seemed not to respond to her sails but only to the white-capped waves. Our boxes and trunks broke loose out of their crates, and were thrown from one side of the vessel to the other. One must witness the havoc such a storm causes on board a vessel to believe it. Kettles, bottles, night-chambers, and everything not nailed down rolled from port to starboard. The wind varied—now it died down a little but soon returned with unabated fury. There was much rain until June 15.

Meantime the Hollanders quarreled with the German over the time they could cook their food. But these differences did not amount to much. As soon as the helmsman heard of it, he ordered that each of the two groups should be first on alternate days and anyone who ignored this rule should help clean up the deck. This worked splendidly, for the ship below was spic-and-span during the rest of the voyage. . . .

June 16. Fair weather. Sea calm. At 6 in the morning a three-masted ship coming from America hove in sight. Late that evening we witnessed an example of effective discipline on board a ship. Our first helmsman, a man of strong character capable of maintaining order, had become well acquainted with the passengers. There was an unmarried German couple on board. The man was a Mr. Smid, the girl was known as Dora. The helmsman had teased them a great deal, but the couple seemed to think the officers would not molest them. Some of the passengers were suspicious of their conduct and informed the helmsman. This evening the helmsman hung up his lantern in the accustomed place and decided to investigate.

Ordering one of the sailors to stand guard, he investigated the sleeping quarters and found the reports were true. With some difficulty the woman was removed from her berth. Mr. Smid was placed in the coalbin in the bow of the ship while Dora was locked up somewhere in the stern, where they remained for the night.

June 17. Very agreeable weather. Unfortunately mother could not come on deck because our little Frederick, who was too young to take any food except his mother's milk, suffered greatly. The poor child cried all day and night.

At 10 o'clock Smid and Dora, the two lovers, were led out of their confinement and brought before the captain. A sailor acted as interpreter. The captain lectured them severely and ordered them to lead a more moral life. Thereupon the couple, being ashamed, were given their freedom, but for several days remained between decks.

In the afternoon the helmsman caught a large fish, a so-called "sea-hog," which provided us with some entertainment. After it was killed, being butchered like a pig, it was cut up and prepared for food. Some of its red meat was salted. The fish fought so vigorously that in being hoisted aboard, its tail struck a privy standing in the bow, hurling it overboard. I was ordered to make a new one, which kept me occupied for some time.

June 18. In the morning agreeable weather, but a contrary wind. Every passenger received a portion of the fish we caught yesterday. We cut it into slices and pounded it much as one prepares beefsteak. We fried the meat with some ham, and the whole including fried potatoes proved very delicious.

Toward evening one of the sailors was placed in confinement. He had been talking with one of the passengers, which was against the rules of the ship. When the officers took him to task for it, he became saucy and insulting. . . .

June 23. Fair weather, the ship was steady. In the evening the Germans fittingly celebrated Saint John's Day, which also was the twenty-fifth birthday of one of their group. This man was escorted to the aft deck where his sister presented him with a bottle of Rhenish wine, of which they had a plentiful supply. In the neck of the bottle was placed a palm branch to which were tied a piece of sausage, a lemon, some dried prunes, etc. After having given him our congratulations, we all drank his health with many bottles of beer which the captain had in store. We also proposed a toast to the captain, the officers of the ship, and in fact everybody and everything. That evening we learned how the Germans surpassed all other peoples at singing. . . .

July 4. Declaration of Independence, which is celebrated by every American. So did we. Early in the morning flags were run up, and at 8 the crew fired salutes. One man who had been a dealer in fireworks got permission to open a box of guns. Everybody who had a liking for shooting could do so as much of it as he wished. At 10 one of the pigs was distributed among the passengers. Saw many fish, also a ship. We had a fresh breeze; the evening was fair but cold. At the request of Mr. Westven, the captain gave the Hollanders permission to sing psalms. The captain sang the last psalm with us. We were approaching the Newfoundland Banks.

July 5. Weather very cold. Captain and helmsman with instruments making observations from the rigging. At dawn the helmsman awoke Snoeps and me to show us an iceberg we had expressed a desire to see. We could see it plainly without the aid of instruments. The day was cold, but the men remained on deck all day in order to see the icebergs that lay on both sides of our ship. One of the icebergs had the form of a village church. The officers estimated the last one we passed was about 160 feet high. We were struck with awe beholding these vast masses of ice gleaming in the sunlight and silently floating by. I shuddered when I thought of the great danger those icebergs were to the ships that crossed their path. We saw many large fish spouting water and believed they were whales. The air was cold, but we had a beautiful night. The officers placed a lantern at the bow and kept watch. . . .

July 8 and 9. Nothing new. Wind steady but from the west and south-west. The delicacies we had been eating from the beginning of the voyage were nearly gone. Also sugar and vinegar were nearly exhausted. Potatoes became worse each day and drinking water was becoming brackish. Everybody was tired of peas and beans. . . .

July 22. Warm weather, and suffocating below deck. Little or no breeze. We were excited and could scarcely sleep. At about 11 o'clock A.M. we dropped anchor. Opposite, in Boston Bay, an island with the quarantine station on it. Here we were to remain all day until given orders. All useless objects were discarded. The helmsman even threw overboard some of the wooden shoes and caps belonging to the girls from Goes and Zierikzee. We were ordered to clean up everything and scrub the deck below, and make ourselves presentable. Next morning we put on our best clothes. The health officers came aboard early and examined everyone. They complimented the captain and officers on the cleanliness of ship and passengers, and took the captain with them to the island. After an hour our captain returned. Loud hurrahs went up from all of us; hats and handkerchiefs were waved, and he literally was carried from the boat into the cabin, visibly pleased with the ovation. Soon a tug appeared to bring our ship into the bay on which the city of Boston is built.[10]

> Mathias Duerst, a Swiss colonist, emigrated to New Glarus, Wisconsin, with his wife and two small children in 1845. This selection from Mathias's diary, which was originally written in German, shows the hardships of the Atlantic crossing. The immigrants on board the ship not only endured inedible food and seasickness, but also the deaths of fellow passengers.

At nine o'clock of the morning of the 13th we pushed from the shore; an hour was spent in getting us into proper position with ropes and windlass; then our ship was taken in tow by a steamer which is always ready in the harbor for that purpose. At ten o'clock we moved off and bade farewell to Europe, perhaps forever for many of us. The steamer pulled us out about two leagues when we were given over to wind and waves. Seasickness took possession of most of us, and there was vomiting all around, none of us could remain on our feet even those who escaped the sickness, because of the heavy rolling of the ship by the waves. So we sailed with variable winds until Wednesday the 21st when there came a storm that drove the sweat out of the pores of many of us. Although the distance from the ships rail to the surface of the water was at least 16 feet and certainly the vessel reached a like number of feet under the surface, yet the ship lay now on this, now on the other side until the rail dipped into the water. The storm ceased on the morning of the 22d; the wind was completely still so that the ship made only two leagues this day. On the 23d we made better progress and on the 24th yet better, but the 25th was for us again a day of terror; a storm arose in the night, which reigned the whole following day with terrible madness. Many a one sobbed Oh if I had only remained in my home. From the 24th until the 26th Noon we were not allowed to make any fire, neither for the grown or the little could anything warm be cooked; those who had bought some food on land, cheese, or crackers could get along, but I and many others must fast, for the ships provisions seem contrived not entirely to kill human beings yet to make them very sick; much of it could not be eaten. The meat is all packed in barrels and so much salted that we have to wash it many times then parboil it and again throw the water away until it was fresher, but even then it was hardly edible. We receive 2 ½ lbs per week to each adult person; those under 12 years were reckoned two for one. Hard tack we have sufficient but this is not a human food. The pigs that are kept on ship refuse to eat it; it is in ¼ lb pieces and of a dark brown color inside and out, and so hard as to require a hammer to break it up in pieces; it is made solely of bran and only a wolfs stomach can digest [it]; it is calculated to kill by slow starvation. The rice is also of the worst quality, yet it is edible; each person gets ½ lb weekly. Beans and peas are fair. Butter as I have described it. Flour was gritty with sand and ½ lb per week was a portion for each. Potatoes were very bad, black, bad smelling and rotten, hardly fit for pigs. Such as they were we got but sparingly of them, sometimes none for 3 or 4 days. We often wished for some of ours at home. The water is rain water several weeks old and leaves a black sediment after standing awhile; but we had enough of it and that we were thankful for. After recovering from seasickness one gets a thirst that can hardly be quenched; one should have acid dried fruits in such cases, which is better than all the medicine is the world. We greatly wished for our Green Sap Sago cheese [Schabzieger] to give a better flavor to our rancid watery potatoes and to strengthen our stomachs. One should take along sugar and coffee also, especially those who contract their passage with the ship food included. I advise—from experience—every person or company that may follow us either on their own account or under control of any society, to bring their own supply of food if they value their health, besides it is ⅓ cheaper. The agents in Amsterdam, Sambrie & Co., make a profit of 29 florins on each passenger, which on the 185 expedited by them on this ship makes 4,495 florins. We have such miserable food that God may pity us. I only wish that those who so miserably contracted us might have the power to glance into this hospital; they would blush in terror on their own account. I would not wish my worst enemy the condition we are in. I trust we will get double reward, for we have passed through purgatory. I believe I could defy seasickness, and actually escaped the vomiting, but an excessive dysentery is wasting my flesh and strength. And I am not the only one, the strongest constitutions that seemed to defy all changes of food and water heretofore do not escape this evil. This condition we ascribe to the use of unaccustomed food; had we smoked meat instead of salted we would not have suffered so.

On the 28th we realized the results of our bad lot; we sorrowed over two victims, Anna Beglinger, [who was] Rudolf Stauffacher's wife of Matt. [a village in Switzerland] after suffering many deaths for several days gave up her spirit this afternoon at 3 Oclock. She was wrapped and sewed into a large linen sheet; three pails full of sand were placed at her feet so as to sink her body. We carried her on deck laid her on a plank, we sang the first two verses of the 140 hymn, Leader Grob read our home funeral service, and so one hour after her death she was sunk into the ocean, where she will undergo no decay, and her bones need not first be sought and gathered at the resurrection. After she had sunk, the remaining verses of the hymn were sung; all of the ships people were on deck, and Leader Grob made a touching address, and urged us to be patient and united. Fruitless words; even when the water rises to and into the lips of the Glarus people they will not leave off their hatred, envy, distrust and self-love, each follows only his own lead; to be just, there are exceptions, but they are the grains of Gold in the sand on the shores. On the same day at 7 P.M. the ½ year old child of Henry Stauffacher of Matt. died, it was bound into a pillow and placed over night in a small boat on deck, and next morning the 29th committed to the waves with like services as before; we sang the 142 hymn. This day we again had storm, but our fear was not now so great because we were more accustomed to it, and we knew that there was not much danger even with great storms on the high sea, unless they become cyclones and raise great masses of water out of the sea to great heights and carry it along many leagues. Should a ship have the misfortune to be in its path it is helplessly lost; they are termed waterspouts; we saw none such.

On the morn of the 30th the storm quieted down and we had fine weather and good wind all day.

The 31st was a splendid day with bright sunshine, we sailed 50 to 60 leagues in 12 hours. This fore noon at 10 our ship had sailed just half the distance of our voyage, the other half we might make with favorable winds in 10 or 12 days; but it might take 20 or 30. So we passed the joyous month of May on the water where no blossoms or flowers perfume the air, but where we suffered fear, sorrow and pain, with but few joys between. Only a firm confidence in God, and the hope that over there in America a better future smiles upon us inspires and keeps us from despair. . . .

On the 17th had some wind, and on the 18th still better. We believe and hope to see land if the wind remains so favorable until next morning. We have so much more cause to long for the desired shore because this day our principal food, the potatoes, were all consumed, and we fear we shall suffer hunger if fate keeps us much longer on the Sea. For one can hardly support life with the portions of other food given us. We could have had potatoes for a much longer time if they had been sound at first. They rotted in the hold and a terrible stench arises from them; it is as if there was a rotting manure heap and yet so driven by want were we that we ventured at the disgusting work of sorting and picking out the few sound ones from the rotten mass. We had now to make use of the horse food otherwise known as hard tack [Zweiback] already described, and I look on with a sad smile to see human beings for hours whetting their teeth in endeavor to bite and chew it; those who possessed good teeth got along fairly but those not so fortunate would get hungrier as they tried to chew it. It filled the stomach but contained little nutriment. 19th the hope to see land this morning was not fulfilled although we sailed well all night. It is now again nearly complete calm. A few days since we made an unpleasant discovery which very much increased our longing to get on land. I hardly dare to write it; body lice in great number have shown themselves on some of the less cleanly, and it is feared that they will so spread as to infest all of the passengers unless all possible preventive means are taken. It would be anything but a pleasant companionship. For this reason I at once had my long hair cut, for as soon as I heard of the presence of these unclean guests I imagined I was infested, but to my joy the fear was groundless. The one who bred this unwelcome population was from the proud town of Ennenda, his name is * * * It is well that it was none of our Valley people or we would have great censure.

This evening the little son Rudolf of Henry Hoesli of Diessbach died; he declined a long time and suffered from convulsions. It was sad to see him when sick and not be able to give him any relief. He was on the morning of the 20th with the customary services committed to the waves; we sang the 138 Hymn. Myself and every feeling person can imagine how painful it must be for parents who have loved a child to commit it to the watery elements. We that were born and brought up on the land are unused to such disposition. We think it more comforting to entrust our dead to mother earth on firm land, but when one considers that the water as well as the land is a creation of God and that finally on the day of judgement the reward follows the deeds, then it can make no difference when, where, or how, we must die. If we have only lived so as to be ready, it is well. The goodness of God made itself evident in the case of Barbara, the mother of the dead child; her husband confined to his bed by sickness could give her no assistance in the care of the child. Other friends were weak and seasick and she alone had to watch and care for the dying one, many a time when no one else could venture on deck in the fierce storm, in greatest danger of being thrown down and washed overboard, she went to cook some warm food for her beloved child. This day we again got along swiftly, the wind blew strong and steady from the rear, and I just have heard the report that the Captain has said that even with moderately favorable wind we would see land tomorrow afternoon. How glad we would be if it prove true.

On the 21st our hope is again cheated. No America in sight yet. I have determined to believe no more reports; what the eyes see the heart believes. I shall trust only my own eyes. This afternoon it rained harder than I ever saw it before; it ran in streams for an hour, and it was sultry to suffocation, all of the passengers below crowded for air to the openings. It is remarkable to notice for us, that the days are fully three hours shorter than at home. In the longest days in Glarus it is lighter at 2 A.M. than here at 4 A.M. At 8 in the evening it is already night, and that impresses even an uneducated person that there is not such a great difference between the longest and shortest days as in Switzerland.

On the 22nd again a weary Sunday. The people at home are no doubt walking through fields and meadows, stretching the potato tops to mark their growth. In our thoughts we wish ourselves there for a few hours. Weak winds in the morning, stronger in the afternoon, still no land in sight. On the 23rd a heavy storm tossed us around considerably. On the 24th a ship coming from America came at a signal from our Captain so near that they could speak with trumpets with each other. I could not understand English but gathered that the ship was bound for France. Many people were on board. Afternoon another met and passed us. The splendid wind chased our ship through the waves like the best steamer, let us see if there is nothing new in sight by morning. 25th and 26th both days nearly total calm, so near to land and not be able to move from the spot is nearly unendurable.

The 27th the most joyful day of the whole ocean voyage; about 10 A.M. a coasting vessel came up and they asked our Captain if we were in want of provisions. I presume the Captain answered he was not for the boat left us again. About 11 o'clock the joyful cry Land! was heard. All who were not already on deck streamed up, myself among the latter, and really we saw what resembled a row of great trees. The American flag was at once hoisted on the foremast; every body expressed their gladness and thanked God, and I believe most sincerely from their hearts, for whoever has lived through 46 days of such misery, even the most hardened is glad to be redeemed. We waited with impatience until the expected pilot should come who was to guide our ship to the coast. At last we saw a coast vessel approach us with lightning speed and at 6 P.M. the man boarded our ship; the boat that brought him turned and with all speed departed leaving us way behind in a short time. No one who has not had our experience can imagine what enthusiasm reigned among our people; the faces were all changed, and one could read joy and gladness in them all. At once all our privations and troubles seemed forgotten.[11]

Having survived the rigors of the Atlantic journey, European immigrants had to decide where they wished to settle and how to get there. Most prospective immigrants received advice and warnings prior to their trip from family and friends living in America, newspaper articles, and even published guides to immigration. In his 1853 German-language guidebook for prospective immigrants, Christian Traugott Ficker not only offered his thoughts on who should emigrate to America, but also included specific directions in getting to Wisconsin. (For background on Ficker and his guide, see pages 8–9). Here, he offers instructions for those unfamiliar with either the English language or American culture journeying from New York to Wisconsin.

In New York there are probably as many official agents as there are states in the union. Each of these is instructed by his government to gain new immigrants for his particular state. Therefore, it cannot be otherwise than that the agent for Michigan, for example, will belittle the State of Wisconsin, or conversely, the Wisconsin agent Michigan. One must pay little attention to them but follow his own ideas and the truthful representations of friends possibly already settled in America, provided he can believe them. As far as I am aware, every region and every condition in America, as in all other countries, has its "but." Yet I have the idea that, at least in the beginning, one should assign great, yes the greatest weight, to the healthfulness of the State in order to accustom himself to the American climate and the great changeableness of the weather. In this respect, with good reasons, I recommend (for Germans) Michigan, Wisconsin, Iowa, Minnesota, and all states lying within these latitudes. Only I have to remark that middle and northern Michigan are very wild and have sandy, infertile land which will not come into cultivation for long, long years. Southern Michigan is very fertile and consequently is already well-settled, and the land is moderately high-priced.

Assuming that the plan is to go to Wisconsin, I shall give the most necessary directions for doing so. At New York go to the responsible agent from Wisconsin (this year he is Mr. H. Haertel) whose residence and office can be ascertained from the German society. He has the strictest orders from his government to be helpful *ex officio* to those who come to him intending to journey to Wisconsin; to give them advice regarding the best and cheapest mode of travel, and to protect them as far as possible from being cheated. Also, one can go to the German society to receive suggestions about a firm that will undertake to forward his goods to Milwaukee. Just this moment my neighbor, the veterinarian, John of Rochlitz, said to me that he had been moved to Milwaukee very fairly and cheaply by a certain Mr. Wolf, a forwarder near the German society in New York. I would advise that several combine and make a bargain in common, because in this way one can easily secure some concession in price. In bargaining, however, let it be clearly understood that one is to be forwarded by steam only from New York via Albany, Buffalo, Detroit, New Buffalo, Chicago, to Milwaukee. From New York you go by steamboat to Albany, and thence to Buffalo by railway. Don't permit yourself to be misled into going by canal

EMIGRANT-LANDING IN NEW YORK.

An immigrant's first encounter with America was usually the bustling waterfront of New York City. *Harper's Weekly*, June 26, 1858. WHI IMAGE ID 79119

under the impression that it is cheaper. The cheapness only appears so, for the little one saves is expended doubly in the greater duration of the journey since by rail one goes from Albany to Buffalo in about thirty-six hours while by canal it often takes as much as fourteen days and longer. It often happens, on this account, that passengers leave the canal boat midway and take the train, preferring to lose the passage money already paid.[12]

> After arriving in America, the family of Mathias Duerst had to arrange for overland passage to Wisconsin. The Duersts and their fellow Swiss settlers took the Pennsylvania Railroad to the Ohio River and then steamed by boat to St. Louis. Duerst's account, which was written in German, begins as the group arrives at the Mississippi River. Duerst was a member of a small party of young men that was sent north to find fertile land for settlement.

The 22nd [July, 1845]. Today about 10 A.M. we steamed into the Mississippi, the water is very muddy and full of drift wood, just like the forest torrents after a heavy rain. If I could wish all the wood I see stranded on the sand bars, into the parish of Diessbach, they would have no need for many years to distribute their Beech parcels. Likewise if I could distribute to our poor at home all of the food that is thrown away on the steamers, we would need no poorhouse or poor act, for no food is served the second time—all that is not eaten the first time is thrown away, not only on the vessels but also in hotels and dwellings. A proof that there is not only enough, but the greatest overflow in this country. Today the first mate, who speaks German well, requested me to give him a full list of our people. I made him a table according to families and age, and who was to pay full or half fare or were free. . . .

28th. This forenoon we started and it took four hours of hard work to move the boat from the spot. Much of the freight Salt, Whiskey and Sugar had to be loaded on a flat boat. In the night the Mosquitoes tormented us so that we could not close our eyes from night till morning. My hands were all swollen as if I had the worst kind of itch. This evening we asked of the Captain, knowing that there were only two or three cabin passengers, if he could not for a small recompense allow us to sleep in a little room, as we had no bedding at all and had for two nights slept on floors and boxes without a particle of bedding. He let us know that if each paid one dollar he would provide beds for us. Of course we could not accept this, as we were now travelling at the expense of poor families. Thereupon a German, who had however been here over 40 years, gave us some bedding to use. We had hardly laid down when the boat again got stuck. Then arose a terrible thunder storm such as only America can produce. One peal followed an other close. In one respect we were glad of it for we believed the rain would raise the river; for nothing is more annoying than to desire to get along as fast as possible to carry out our mission, and then to be stuck on one spot. . . .

On the 4th my companions Grob and Freuler went out about a mile to engage a farmer if possible who would carry us for less money than the stage, but the farmer had other uses for his horses and another asked 30 dollars. So we found it best to take the stage, where we each paid $3.18. At 8 A.M., we left in an old stage which ought long since to have been retired; besides us three there was a gentleman, his wife and son; we rode in this ancient chest about 16 miles where the horses and stage were changed, but such a miserable conveyance, a farmer's wagon with a torn cover of the kind that gypsies use with us, and a road on which God's mercy was needed; the horses were changed every five hours; for these, it is a pity that they cannot run on a Glarus road. In America everything is the opposite of Switzerland,—here the horses excel those of the noblest lord, but the most miserable beggarly vehicles; there, elegant carriages, but mostly poor mean horses; when the mail arrived at Glarus the horses nearly fell from exhaustion; here, at the end of their stage, one could hardly hold them; there were always four hitched up and we rode the whole day over prairie vast as an ocean; for many miles we could see nothing but the sky and the meadows, no tree, shrub, house or person to be seen; the eye was lost in its immensity; then came the seam of a forest which reminded me of the time when we first saw land from the Ocean. In the vacant land we saw today, all Glarus would have room,—no one uses it, and the grass rots where it grows; the roads are very poor, when one track becomes worn or impassible another is made alongside so that often 3, 4 or more tracks are thus made. At 6 P.M. we arrived at the village of Stepton [Illinois], on the Rock River; here we got another driver and changed horses but not wagons; after riding six miles the whole outfit was ferried across the river to the village of Grand Detour, where we spent the night in the stage station for which we paid a dollar for all three, without breakfast.

. . . But we left here this 8th of August at 7 ½ A.M. and rode all the time until afternoon, when our teamster switched off to the right and drove a couple of miles through a valley, where we finally came to a log house and saw again human beings the first since morning. Our teamster made inquiries and ascertained that they were yet 2 miles further on; again we proceeded to another house, there our driver halted and would go no farther. We however prevailed upon him to at least go with us on foot and show us the direction to take, for there was neither track nor road. A boy showed us along a piece further in the proper direction, until we saw men. Grob and I had taken another direction, but had to turn back because we could not cross the creek which flows through our land and which swarms with good fish. Judge Duerst and Mr. Streiff saw us floundering along, and in the supposition that perhaps we were people of their company, they came to meet us. The feelings that then rose in us, I cannot and will not describe. To all of us came the tears of joy. After the excitement of finding each other had subsided in a measure, we went into the huts they had made at first. You may imagine that from both sides came many questions and answers until late at night. They prepared supper for us—Judge Duerst baked the bread. We also the same evening walked a short distance over our land and enjoyed the splendid sight—it is beautiful beyond expectation. Excellent timber, good soil, many fine springs and a stream filled with fish. Water sufficient therein the whole year to drive a mill or saw mill. Wild grapes in abundance. Much game, Deer, Prairie Chicken and Hares, in short all that one could expect. This 8th August is therefore the fortunate day on which we arrived at the glad certainty as to the whereabouts of our land and our expert pioneers.[13]

The trip to Wisconsin was completed only after finding a place to live and setting up a home. For both foreign and domestic settlers, establishing a household on the Wisconsin frontier was no easy task. Johann Frederick Diederichs (b. 1804) provides an account of this process in a letter, originally written in German, to his relatives in Milwaukee. A year earlier, Diederichs and his family had traveled from Elberfeld, Germany, to Manitowoc and endured many discomforts on the overseas and overland journey to Wisconsin. However, as this translated excerpt shows, once they settled in Manitowoc, the Diederichs family was optimistic about their new home in America.

Milwaukee

Jan. 3, 1848

. . . After searching for several days we finally found some suitable land, 9 miles from Manitowoc, 7 miles from Rapids, and 20 to 22 miles from Sheboygan. It was decided to build a house on each 160 acres, the same to serve as a temporary residence, and later, when the land should be divided, to be used as a stable. For the time being we were quartered with our nearest neighbor, Hobecker, and started to work immediately— cut down trees for logs, carried them on our shoulders through the snow, which had fallen in the meantime, to the building site, and continued this work from Monday until Saturday, all week long.

If you, my dear ones, could have seen me—how I arose in the morning from my bed of cornstalks with a block of wood for a pillow, partook of half baked or half burnt, sour, dry bread and black coffee without sugar, for breakfast; at noon dry bread and black coffee again, with turnip soup, and the same in the evening—then, I am sure, you would have been nearer tears than laughter. But in these days of hard work, privations, and the overcoming of all disgust, I have found what strength and joyousness come from the knowledge that we are in the path of the Lord. . . .

And now, my dear ones, I am a farmer, have eighty acres or 128 Prussian Morgens of land, and livestock consisting of a dog and a cat. A sturdy peasant—eh? The dog is indispensable on account of the cattle, the cat on account of the mice, which are numerous in the woods. I have fine, rolling land, sloping toward the morning sun, with trees slender and tall, such as oaks of three varieties, sugar or maple, beech, elm, ash, walnut trees, plum trees, etc. Indeed, if I could do as I wished, I should forthwith give you a present of 15,000 to 20,000 dollars; for Pflieps, who is a carpenter, tells me that if any one would pay me $30,000 for my lumber laid down in Elberfeld, he would have a splendid bargain. You may ask what we do with it. Into the fire with the soundest, finest trees, three or four feet in diameter! Into the fire with them if we do not happen to need them for fences or some other purpose. Through the middle of my property flows a little creek, about the size of the Lohrmuehler Creek near Neviges, giving me a layout for the finest pastures. In short, my land is so pretty and its location is so excellent that all my friends insist, and I myself admit, that the best portion fell to me, and although Pflieps offered me $25 if I would trade with him, I will not do so but will keep what the Lord has allotted to me.

When once I have my land secure, then I shall work my way through all right. But how the money goes you may learn from the following: Just now I need a barrel of flour and cannot buy one for less than $7; then I still need four hundred feet of boards, which I must buy, for I cannot afford to saw them myself, since I dare not lose an hour from clearing the land and preparing it for seeding. The more I have for planting and seeding the more shall I have at harvest. I must have potatoes to plant, wheat, oats, and corn to sow, and must have some to live on until harvest. Whatever, therefore, is not absolutely necessary, must be deferred and done without. Hence I dare not think of cows and oxen, necessary and profitable though they would be. But I am sure that if I clear and partly plant from six to eight of my eighty acres by summer, I could easily get from four to five hundred dollars from the same. Then I could pay for the land and have three or four hundred dollars left. But I am heartily tired of roving about and long for rest. If it is the Lord's will, I shall die here, and I hope that such will be His will.

Farms which are well situated and whereon enough has been cleared and planted to support a family are very rapidly rising in price, for during the summer immigrants who have money are arriving nearly every day, and would rather buy a farm than settle on Congress land in the midst of the woods. I venture to say that since there is no Congress land available in or near Milwaukee, the trend of immigration will be toward this place and Sheboygan. This is advantageous to us, for it increases the value of our land and makes it easier to sell our produce.

Follow me now, my dear ones, in my daily work, as it has thus far appeared, and let me lead you into our family life and present to you a picture of our activities and contentment.

Not counting small injuries to our hands, caused by the hard work and rigorous cold, we are all well and happy, for which we cannot sufficiently thank our dear Lord. We arise at daybreak in the morning, about six or half past six, read the Word of God together, and drink coffee, with milk—no, no! Milk? A farmer such as I am does not yet have that, but, as head of the family, I have sugar, which is very cheap here, and probably next year will cost us nothing, for then we can tap it ourselves. With the coffee we have very good bread. With butter perhaps? Where there is no milk there can be no butter, and we should have to be satisfied with dry bread if mother had not saved some bacon fat into which we can dip it.

Directly after breakfast we begin working, and since Kohl is still busy preparing doors and windows for the house, I, with Fred and Carl, each with ax on shoulder, go out to clear the land about the house; we chop the branches off the trees and shorten the trunks as much as possible so that they will not be too heavy to carry or roll to the wood-pile. That is no easy work, and the higher the pile of logs, brush, and chips is, the better it is and the merrier will it burn.

Towards noon we return to the house, and mother has white beans with bacon, or bean soup with bacon, or rice soup with bacon, or barley soup with bacon, or flour dumplings with bacon, which last combination usually constitutes our Sunday meal. Potatoes, vegetables, or beef are for the present not to be found with us, and just now mother reports that there is no more barley left; hence in the future we shall have one course less, and the good housewife will have that much less trouble deciding what to cook.

Then back to work again, accompanied by the good mother and Mrs. Kohl to aid us as well as they can, and after sundown we all repair to the house and treat ourselves again to black coffee, dry bread, and sometimes bacon. Then we read a chapter from the Bible and gather about the warm stove, chat about you and others, venture guesses that this one will follow us and the other also, and that this one will fit in here, and the other not. Often I am so exhausted from the hard day's work that I am too tired to smoke a pipe, for to begin such work at the age of 44 years, and not lose courage, is some undertaking! But I must acknowledge and praise the faithful assistance of my Fred and Carl, and I hope their obedience and diligence will yet bring us much joy. They, as well as their two sisters, have grown considerably. . . .

You will next ask: "Is it really good in America, and are you not sorry that you have gone there?" And I can give you the answer, from my full conviction and in accordance with the truth: "Yes, it really is good here, as well for people with money as for those that have none, if the latter are capable and industrious workmen or mechanics—among whom I include carpenters, especially joiners, shoemakers, blacksmiths, tailors, tinsmiths, etc." The mechanics receive at once, if they are shop foremen, twelve shillings, $1.50 per day, without board, as the owner of a shop in Milwaukee informed me—which, by the way, is said to be one of the worst places for mechanics in America. But every one must see to it that he is thoroughly competent in his line, otherwise it will go hard with him if he must work with Americans. If, however, one intends to become a farmer and has money to buy a farm, he will find here a pleasant life and an assured future awaiting him; daily the finest estates, with cattle and all things that belong thereto, are being sold at from eight hundred to four or five thousand dollars, according as the farm is large or small, much or little cleared, near or far from cities or landing places. As for one who has no money, he will do best first to hire out to a farmer. He can then easily lay by fifty dollars within half a year, and with that he can buy 40 acres of Congress, that is, unimproved, land. Of course he must thoroughly exert himself that his land be made arable and, if he begin in the spring, that it be fruitful the same year; but after he has passed this first year he need have no more anxiety as to subsistence, and ere three or four years have elapsed he will be able to take part of his harvest to any of the numerous markets and exchange it for money or victuals.

As far as hunting is concerned, let no one entertain any false notions, for while there is plenty of game, the newly arrived farmer has more important things to attend to than to spend his time hunting; for he must direct all his activities to clearing and building, and think of other matters only when he has attained a secure position. Self-dependence and endurance must not be wanting in immigrants, especially in those without means. Whoever is faint-hearted and cannot conform to any condition in life, had better not come. The word "distress" is unknown to the Americans. As far as I am concerned, I can, hand on heart, declare naught else but that I thank the Lord that I am here and regret that I did not come sooner; and when my memory turns to many among you and I reflect how, with your means, you could live here, I am sorry, humanly speaking, not to have you here.

Joh. Frederick Diederichs[14]

In 1845, John Hodgson was another recent arrival from Europe faced with the challenge of finding a new home in Wisconsin. In this letter to his parents in Yorkshire, England, Hodgson describes how he settled into his surroundings in rural Iowa County and laments the shortage of women in a country seemingly full of single men.

Reevesville, Wisconsin
June 18, 1845

Dear Parents:

. . . We fell in with lots of emigrants going to Wisconsin. We left our luggage at the Mounds and started off on foot for the English settlement, and I picked up a lot of land, eighty acres which lays in a good place for markets. It is near some of the society farms [i.e., farms belonging to the British Emigration Temperance Society in Mazomanie]. The land appears to be good land but not so level as I would like it but there is a good stream of water running through it and a staked out road. I think you will not like it the first sight. It lays between two bluffs where there is plenty of stone for building and lime. It's the best place in the world for keeping stock for there is no person can come in behind us. . . .

William has not got employ but we could both have got employ about 40 miles from Milwaukee. We are 120 miles from the latter. We have made a shanty to live in and we have got the logs cut to build a log home and we intend getting it raised when we get them hauled. I have bought one yoke of oxen. They cost 41 dollars and I think of buying a cow. They can buy very nice ones with a calf for about 50 shillings. This is not a very good place for young men as they are new settlers but a few miles off there is plenty of work and cash but there will be plenty of it here after a while. We are going to fence and improve the land. The neighbors will help us to raise the house ready when you come and I would have you come out this fall and as early as you possibly can for we shall not be very well off without a housekeeper. I would have you come out but do not have too high notions for if you expect too great things you may have a fall but I should be very happy if you were here. But you need not tell my girl not to come for girls are very scarce here. They are all batchelors around about us. I hope we shall do first rate after a while but we must expect troubles. We beat about 30 families of the society one of which was Mr. Hanly that started off from home the week before us. You must tell Tho. Atkinson we beat him ten days and had a great deal more comfortable voyage, they having 300 passengers we 30 so you may query there may not be so many coming out in the fall, so it will be cheaper than in the spring. You may come this fall and get here early if you come by New Orleans. Then up the Mississippi by boat as far as Galena. They are mining lead there.

Be careful not to have too many pounds of luggage and bring as few new clothes as you can do without, don't lay your money out useless. You will have to pay money on new clothes. You must bring some small fish hooks. We have fish in the creeks and plenty of deer, prairie hen, pigeons and all kinds of birds. In fact the country is not lied about only people do not expect too great things but what can you expect of a place that three years ago there was not a house within ten miles. But it is a fine healthy country and we are seven miles from a mill.

I shall not have time to write any more before you come so you must write as soon as you can. I am sending a letter to my intended so you must let her see this. She may want to write back when you do. I should have sent hers in one. There would have been less to pay. You must make up your mind to over come difficulties if you intend to come along. Any person coming having money to spare can do well to buy cows. They will do the best of anything. It is too late to plant anything this season but I hope we shall have something to reap another harvest after this. You need not bring your oven they use stoves in this country. I would come to meet you at New York but my expenses would buy a cow and then the loss of time too. There is no place that has been so quickly settled as this place. They are coming in from all the other states so it seems to me that it is a fine country. Young men can get good wages and room and board at Mineral Point for digging lead. You must give my respects to friends. Tell them I am in good health. And I hope this will find all well. Tell them I could be very much at home if I could have a Misses around. Well, a man is free here and there are several rich widows. I am the poorest man in the territory. You might bring a flock of lassies.

No more from your dutiful son,
John Hodgson[15]

What began as an idea turned into a journey and eventually resulted in a new home and way of life. Wisconsin pioneers varied in terms of their ethnicity, language, skills, and age. Some encountered a difficult journey; others thought of it as a great adventure. What they all shared were dreams and hopes as they tried to adapt to a new place.

2

"HIGH HOPES THAT WE SHOULD BE HAPPY"

Adjusting to a New Land

New settlers, whether American- or European-born, did not simply recreate their old lives anew on arriving in Wisconsin. They immediately faced challenges: some of them environmental, others cultural. Wisconsin's climate differed from what settlers had been accustomed to in their old homes. Sickness and death plagued pioneer families in an era when medical knowledge was still primitive. Some reported loneliness, boredom, and feelings that today would be classified as depression. One schoolteacher expressed sheer exhilaration upon the end of the school year but then longingly noted how much she missed her students. Another woman, abandoned by her husband who failed to leave her with any money, asked the legislature for release from the marriage through divorce. Some settlers embraced changes with enthusiasm; others regretted leaving their homes and were disillusioned with the promises of life in Wisconsin. Most suffered from deep homesickness and missed friends and relatives who lived far away.

The most immediate challenge that many settlers faced was the weather. Wisconsin's cold winters and hot summers were not for the faint-hearted. Although many settlers were already somewhat accustomed to severe climates, others found Wisconsin weather very difficult to bear. In his 1853 German-language guide for immigrants,

Christian Traugott Ficker warns prospective settlers from Germany about the different weather they will face once they arrive in their new homeland. (For background on Ficker and his guide, see pages 8–9.)

The climate of Wisconsin in general is the same as that of New York and New England, yet here the atmosphere is drier, clearer, and therefore also more healthful than there, which advantage is also affirmed for Indiana, Illinois, Missouri, and so on. Wisconsin up to the present is held to be the most healthful of the western states. It is true that the heat in summer is often pretty oppressive as the winter cold is pretty severe. Still, I can find no particular difference between the climate here and the climate of the Lommatzsch region in Saxony, for there also the summer was often quite oppressive and the winter very cold. I have been in this country five years. The first winter, 1848–49, began in November. There was a rather deep snow, and for thirteen weeks we had uninterruptedly the most perfect sleighing. The following years, however, there was little snow and no persistent cold. The last winter, 1852–53, was the mildest of all with almost no snow and but little frost. Also, there was no second winter. Still, these are merely exceptions. This much is certain: that our winters would not be nearly so severe if it were not for the occasional very piercing, cutting north and northwest winds. When the wind ceases, the severe cold is usually over. It is peculiar that the intense winter cold, as also rainy weather in summer, rarely continues here more than three days. The weather here, as in almost the whole of North America, is extraordinarily changeable. At the moment, when one is almost overcome by the heat, there may come a cool, often a too cool, wind which makes one shiver. That this has a very bad effect upon those who are not accustomed to it is easily seen, for which reason also I recommend to every new immigrant that, particularly at first, he should wear next to the skin both summer and winter a woolen shirt whereby he will in most cases prevent taking cold.

Another peculiarity is the long, beautiful fall and the late spring, as well as the usually late and early frosts. Here the fall is glorious and unquestionably the most beautiful season of all. Still, it usually freezes several times by Michaelmas [September 29] after which we have the most perfect weather. One soon realizes that these frosts cause great damage to tender plants. Also in spring, frosts usually continue long so that here, for example, one does not dare to plant lettuce, cucumbers, and so on, in the garden as early as we do in Germany. One would risk their complete destruction. It is commonly believed (and I think on good grounds) that these late and early frosts will gradually disappear the more the forest is cut down and cleared away and the land becomes open so that the air has free course over the soil to dry it out. Even now it is pointed out that there is a great difference to be seen between the present and earlier years. Who is not aware that in olden times Germany was in the same condition?

Such a beautiful spring as one has in Germany, the cold diminishing in proportion to the ascent of the sun, we rarely know here. Only this year (1853) an exception occurred. Generally the days are comfortable here in March, but the nights cold so that there is often heavy frost. Thus, it continues up to the end of April or the beginning of May. Now suddenly—often in a single night—all trees become green, and hot weather comes on quickly. The farther south the location, the earlier this occurs—farther north, naturally it is longer delayed.

When spring finally begins here, it is almost unbelievable how fast everything grows. At the beginning of the month of May when in the Lommatzsch region they are already cutting clover, when grain is often already heading out, nothing of this sort is as yet to be thought of here; nevertheless, by the beginning or the middle of July harvest is upon us. Whether or not this also will change after many, many years only God knows.[16]

In addition to the rapid swing from warm to cold conditions, new settlers faced potential catastrophes such as floods, prairie fires, tornadoes, and thunderstorms. Edwin and Martha Bottomley and their five children emigrated from England to the town of Rochester in western Racine County in the spring of 1842. Edwin, then thirty-two years old, had earned a good living as a skilled patternmaker for a woolen mill in England, but after realizing that their children were destined to work in a factory, the Bottomleys decided to build a better future in America. In this excerpt from a letter to their friends and family back in England, the Bottomleys describe not only Wisconsin's climate, but also some of the dangers awaiting unwary setters. The unusually spelled words (for example, "depictade" for "depicted" or "blakned" for "blackened") and lack of sentence breaks make this letter difficult to read. For the convenience of the reader, the spelling has been silently corrected here and the first word of each sentence has been capitalized.

Rochester, [Wisconsin]
November 25th 1842

Dear Father & Mother Likewise Br Henry And all relations and Friends

. . . I will now give you a Description of the Climate as well as I can. But as I have no thermometer you must not expect me stating the temperature in degrees. For the first 3 months the weather was rather warmer than it is in England the Sun Shining with great Splendor and the air very pure. The changes from fair to rain are more sudden than with you after a fortnight or three weeks of fine weather with a Sky as clear as Crystal the atmosphere Becomes suddenly filled with clouds Big with rain and electrical fluid when it Bursts forth with tremendous violence the lightning flashing through the clouds with awful grandeur and the thunder Bursting forth with a noise that makes the earth tremble at its violence the rain Pouring down in torrents for 3 or 4 hours when it will cease and the sun will Burst forth and Shine as before. Such was the weather till the latter end of September when we had warm Days and frosty nights which withers the vegetation very fast and causes it to burn with a Swiftness indescribable at the time when the fire sweeps over the country, which generally takes place the latter end of October.

The fire Broke out in this neighborhood on the 26th of October the wind Blowing from the west and Driving the fire in an Easterly Direction about a half a mile on the South side of our house. On the 27th just after we had got our Dinner while George & me were getting a pipe of tobacco our Ruth came running into the house with terror Depicted in her countenance and saying that the fire was coming towards the hay Stack. We immediately ran out and saw that it was and the wind was Blowing from the South with a strong Breeze and Driving the fire Before it right towards our house and Hay Stack and was as much as James Tinker, Squire Hienchlife, George and myself and the women could do to Save them By Beating the fire out with Boughs and throwing water on the ground. No sooner had we got ours safe than we had to run to Jas Tinkers to save the house and Stack and from there to Scotts. The fire continued with unabated fury all that day and night illuminating the Heavens and we could when the night set in see it from our Door in lines of 2 or 3 miles in length Driving away towards the north leaving trees Burning Behind it which stood like burning beacons in the Blackened Space for Several Days and then fell with a tremendous crash. We had taken the precaution to Burn round our stacks but the Dead leaves had fallen on it and had the fire come in the night Both Stacks and Houses would most likely have been Destroyed.

Martha Bottomley, Daguerreotype, ca. 1859–1864.
WHI IMAGE ID 123666

Winter has set in sooner than usual and the ground is now covered with snow and the Frost is very keen and would be called very cold weather with you. Our house is not one of the Best for keeping the snow out and frost for we get snowed on in bed which [when it] is heavy weather and when we get up in a morning we have to pull our shoes off the floor By main force for they freeze to the floor very soon with having nails in them. But we can stop at home while we get our Breakfast Before we turn out to work and come in again when we do not like it.

Edwin & Martha Bottomley[17]

Although the climate presented an obstacle to many families looking to settle in Wisconsin, boosters in many early communities tried to squelch talk of bad conditions that might inhibit immigration to the growing territory. Many residents of new communities attempted to put a positive spin on Wisconsin's climate, claiming that four inches of snow in November was a sign of a healthful environment, as opposed to the more moderate but damp and dismal weather found in other states. As this excerpt from the November 16, 1839, issue of a Mineral Point newspaper illustrates, boosters could find a silver lining in every dark cloud.

THE FIRST SNOW.—On Saturday morning last, about ten o'clock, it commenced snowing and continued until Sunday morning; since when the weather has been very cold. The ground is now covered with snow to the depth of about 4 inches. The season, so far, with the exception of the last few days, has been remarkably mild and pleasant, and this is the first fall of snow we have had. We observe notices in our exchanges of snow storms in various parts of the Union in the same latitude of Wisconsin, which have the reputation of being much more congenial climes. Nevertheless, our winters, though perhaps somewhat colder, are much more pleasant and healthy. They are uniform throughout—the air clear and bracing. We have none of their half-cold, half-warm, wet, disagreeable, slushy weather; we never hear of persons dying with the consumption, and seldom hear complaints of coughs and colds. The river navigation has continued open sufficiently long to enable our merchants to bring up their supplies, and the cold weather has kept back long enough for our farmers to get in all their crops. Our market is well stocked with groceries and provisions of all kinds; and all are selling at very reasonable prices: so that on this score, we have nothing to complain of, but much to be thankful for.[18]

While settlers found ways to cope with a harsh climate, illness threatened the prosperity and lives of many new immigrants. Largely unaware of the sources of disease, many settlers ascribed climatic causes to their illnesses. In a world without antibiotics or many of the other benefits of modern medicine, sickness was a serious and often deadly affair. Foreign immigrants in particular, having survived the rigors of a long ocean voyage, felt dispirited by the illnesses they encountered in America, and they expressed their dismay in letters sent to their friends and family in Europe. One such example is found in this excerpt from a letter written by Anders Wiig, Brynnild Leqve, and Johannes Wiig to friends in Norway, which was reprinted in the Norwegian newspaper *Bergens Stiftstidende* on July 29, 1841. The letter was originally written in Norwegian.

January 11, 1841

. . . On our arrival, we were extremely dissatisfied, both because it seemed difficult to find employment and because of the climatic diseases raging here. These are fever ache [malaria], bilious fever, and scarlet fever, each of which appears under many forms. Fever ache, the most common and also the longest lasting, seldom kills if it does not develop complications—and this often happens. It is also called the "shakes," because it regularly, depending on its severity, daily or every second or third day, causes a violent shaking both when it abates earlier or resumes later in the day. It weakens the nervous system to such an extent that anyone who has suffered one attack is in danger of another the following year unless he exercises great caution. After five or seven years, according to report, however, patients are quite recovered.

Many die of bilious fever, from which we have all suffered, though in different ways. This ailment upsets the stomach and disturbs the circulation of the blood, and you cannot get well by letting the illness take its course. If you see a competent doctor at once, however, he will usually be able to cure you in a short time. Scarlet fever, from which few people suffer except children, is said to be contagious. It swells and blocks up the throat and, if a doctor is not available, will kill the sufferer in a few days. These diseases are found in Illinois, Indiana, Michigan, Missouri, and Wisconsin, but in varying degrees according to the locations of the several districts, some being almost completely free of them. Areas around rivers are unhealthful everywhere, as are places where canals have been or are being constructed, and, in short, spots where there is stagnant water or that are low-lying and swampy. Besides, you have to remember to take good care of yourself. It is dangerous to work hard in severe heat, to walk around with wet feet, or to get drenched by rain.

... Last summer we heard practically nothing about illness; and everybody agrees that Wisconsin, or the Wisconsin Territory as it is sometimes called, since it has not yet been admitted to the Union, is the most healthful in the United States. No one will catch climatic diseases here unless he undermines his constitution by riotous living. In short, this state is definitely the one we recommend to immigrants.

But although we do not think that anyone who wants to come here should allow himself to be discouraged by fear of illness, and although it is our conviction that every industrious and able-bodied person will make a better living here than in Norway, yet our purpose is not to persuade anyone to come out here. Rather we would dissuade those who are already making a good living. For people's tastes and ways of thinking are so different that it is impossible to say with certainty that everybody would be happy here. But we do affirm that we have heard no one say that he wished he were back, except Sjur Jørgensen who, against the wish of his wife, set his mind on this—a most peculiar decision in the opinion of all Norwegians here.[19]

> Frontier families, such as the Bottomleys with their five children, found that they could do little for their offspring when illness struck the household. This excerpt from a letter from Edwin and Martha to their family in England shows how a child's fever could quickly develop into a life or death situation. As with the Bottomleys' letter on pages 53–56, the spelling in this excerpt has been silently corrected and the first word of each sentence has been capitalized.

Rochester Racine County W[isconsin] T[erritory]
October 15th 1847

Dear Father:

I am again permitted through the mercy of God to write again to you and I hope this will find you in the enjoyment of good health. Since I wrote last to you our Ruth and Cecelia have both had the ague. All the rest of us are well. Both of them are a Deal better than what they have been and I think with a little care will soon be right. Cecelia began with fits at the first but I think they were caused by her teeth as she was about cutting some at the time. The first fit she had she begun about 12 o'Clock at noon and she continued in It while about 4 o'Clock in the afternoon. We all of us thought she would have Died in it. Her left arm and leg were convulsed and her eyes and mouth Drawn to the left side also while her right side was of a Deathly appearance. We got mustard plasters to her feet as quick as we could and we gave her a few Drops of oil of mint. I would have given her a little tincture of asafetida [a spice used for digestive problems as well as for treating convulsions] if we had had any but we were without and through the blessing of god the means we used proved of service. She had several fits after but none as bad as the first. They came on every other Day gaining three hours every time growing Slighter every time till they ended in the ague. She is now nearly well.

The boy that I have has had the ague and has only been able to work about a fortnight this 8 week which happened rather unfortunate for me. . . .

your affectionate Son & Daughter
Edwin and Martha Bottomley[20]

Illness, of course, did not strike only children in frontier households. When parents succumbed to disease, the result could be both physically and emotionally devastating. The tragedies affected not only the immediate family, but also the victims' kin and friends. James Tinker—a friend of Edwin and Martha Bottomley—vividly portrays the distress that could consume a family when both parents were stricken with a debilitating disease. Tinker addresses the letters to Thomas Bottomley in England, who was Edwin's father.

Rochester Racine Co[un]ty
Octr 6th 1850

Mr Thos Bottomley

Sir: It is with feelings and emotions of a very painful character that I communicate to you, (at the request of your son Edwin) the mournful intelligence, that Edwin and family are at present "wading through the deep waters of affliction". The family is afflicted with the desease here termed "Typhoid fever". Ruth was the first victim whom it attacked. She was first seized with the complaint about six weeks ago. I am happy to say however, that she is now convalescent, and able to sit up some, but so weak and reduced, that it must take some time to restore her to her usual health and strength. Edwin was the next sufferer. it is about two weeks since he was seriously afflicted, and he is stile in a precarious condition. And next Martha, the wife, and mother, with the unremiting care, attendance, & anxiety and the constant watchings and labour, broke down, and had to take to bed, a few days ago so that at present there are three persons, afflicted, in one house, comprising the heads of the family. Now Sir I need not enter into details, and attempt to describe the mournful consequences resulting from this pitiable and unhappy state of affairs. this you can readily immagine. In a large family, when *both* the *heads* are laid low by desease, and incapacitated from attending to their duties, the result cannot be otherwise than distressing in the extreme. Be assured Sir that it is not my design to give additional & unnecessary pain by representing things worse than they really are.

I have written these lines at intervals while waking and watching with your son Edwin. Hannah and her husband are here. Ruth as I before observed is recovering, and I fervently hope that Martha the mother, may not be so seriously afflicted, as Edwin, the father is at present. I would fain hope that Martha's disorder is nothing more serious than physical prostration caused by a lack of natural rest and over-exertion. However it cannot be denied that this "Typhoid fever" is somewhat similar in its nature, symptoms, and results to the "ship-fever" and when it once attacks one member of a family it is extremely likely to [attack] the whole—or at least that portion who may be pre-disposed at the time to catch the desease. Let us hope that the worst is past. The doctor told me this morning, that although Edwin could not be considered altogether free from danger, yet his symptoms were decidedly favourable; and he thought he would recover. Let us then hope for the best. Edwin would have defered writing a little longer, to see how things turned, but he was afraid that George Gill would get to England & see you before you got a letter, and as Ruth had been sick for some time before Geo left, and as Edwin was far from well at the time, he was afraid that if you did not receve a letter you would be getting very eneasy and anxious.

When you see my Father would you be kind enough to give him our kind love, & inform him that at present we are all in moderate health. Tell him also that I am expecting a letter from him. And with best wishes for your health and prosperity, I subscribe myself

Yours Respectfully
[James Tinker]

Rochester, [Wisconsin]
Novr 19th 1850

To Mr T. Bottomley

Dear Sir: I take up my pen once more to communicate to you the mournful details of the continued suffering of your Son Edwin's family. In my last I think I told you of the sickness of Ruth, & Edwin & Martha & Thomas. I am happy to say that Ruth is restored to her usual health and is able to attend upon the others. Martha and Thomas are also improving, being able to sit up a little occasionally. About 12 days back your son Edwin was considered as improving. At that time I had a letter partially written to my father but in consequence of Edwin manifesting symptoms of a relapse I defered posting that letter untill I could communicate some thing posative in the case. I can now do so. And I do assure you that it is with feelings the Keenest anguish that I report the painful fact of the decease of your son Edwin. Edwin was reduced by the first attack to a mere skeleton, & his nervous system was completely shaken; and hence the vital principal was too enfeabled to sustain successfully a Second attack. After this relapse he gradually sunk under the power of the fever. For the last week every day was expected to be the last. I believe he Suffered little or no pain, for when asked how he felt his invariable reply was "first rate." During the latter part of his sickness he wandered considerable. He often immagined that you were present and gave directions providing for your entertainment &

comfort. He frequently addressed himself to his father, and carried on the conversation as if you were present. He lingered on in this way untill last Sundy the 17th inst [i.e., this month] at 2 ½ O Clock P. M. when the vital spark became extinct and he quietly fell asleep without a struggle. Edwin lived the life of the upright, and his end was peace. I assure you that Edwin was universally esteemed by all who had the pleasure of his acquaintance. And this mysterious dispensation of Providence will be regarded as a sore affliction, not only by his large, suffering, and bereaved family; but also by a numerous circle of friends & acquaintances. I never saw such an expression of sympathy as has been exhibited by the neighbors, during the sickness of Edwin. His death is regarded as a public & general loss. But our loss is unquestionably his gain, & therefore we ought not to mourn as those without hope. He has "fought the good fight he has finished his course, and he has gone to receive the crown of his reward." God grant that we all may be prepared to meet him amidst that glorious company of Saints, who throng the courts of Heaven—Amen. The funeral took place yesterday the 18th inst at 2 O Clock P.M. The officiating Minister was the Rev. Mr. Drummond who improved the occasion by preaching a very impressive discourse. There was a very large attendance at the funeral—the Meeting House was completely filled. I never saw such a general and universal exhibition of sorrow, manifested at the funeral of a private individual before.

But I must leave this mournful subject; in order to give you some account of his still suffering family. For further particulars I must refer you to the accompanying letter to my father who will no doubt furnish you with the same.

I am sorry to inform you that since I last wrote M. Beaumont, Wm Schofield, Thos Brown and his wife, your grand-daughter Hannah, are laid low with the fever. The distressing fact cannot be concealed that the house at present is more crowded with the suffering victims of decease than a regular hospital. And no one can fore see the end. Thos Bottomley & William S. are gradually improving. M. Beaumont is also convalescent. one week ago last Sunday we brought Mathew down to our house to make a little more room for the rest. But his place was soon occupied by your grand-daughter Hannah. Last Thursday evening, Hannah was confined and delivered of a fine daughter. All things considered she is at present going on very favourably. Edwin was permitted to see and able to recognize his little grand-child before he died. Martha is also improving. she is able to sit up a little occasionally. But as might be expected, the recent afflictive despensation of Providence in taking away the Partner of her bosom—the husband of her youth, has sorely tried her spirits. God help her! she is wading through the deep waters of affliction. She is left with a large family of fatherless children one half of whom are prostrated by desease! Oh! the prospect is dark and dreary. the family are the victims of desease—their head is cut off in his manhood—their supporter their comforter & their guide is laid low in the cold tomb, and the mother is left to battle with the trials, and hardships of a selfish world alone. I must say considering all the circumstances, she bears up wonderfully. And I can only earnestly repeat the aspiration that the God of Mercy may help her; for I know not to whom she can look for assistance but to the Father of the fatherless, and to yourself!

I am sorry to say that Thos Brown is considered at present, by the Doctors as very dangerous. However he has youth and a good constitution in his favour and we hope for the best. I cannot at present communicate to you any information relative to Edwins private & business affairs. I presume however they will write again, as soon as circumstances will permit. In the mean time they are anxiously expecting a letter from you. I may observe while I think of it that Edwin has made his will and arranged about the disposal of his property. But space forbids my giving you the particulars in this note. I know the facts communicated in this mournful epistle will affect you painfully and I can only pray that God may afford the consolation which He alone can give—I am Respectfully

James [Tinker]
Written at the request of Mrs Bottomley.[21]

In addition to dealing with hot and cold weather, fires, thunderstorms, and life-threatening illnesses, many settlers struggled with the isolation of frontier life. Living and working in a sparsely populated land, miles away from the familiar faces of friends and family, created psychological as well as physical hardships. Soon after accepting the post of federal Indian agent at Prairie du Chien, Joseph Street (ca. 1780–1840) expressed his loneliness in a letter to his brother-in-law, Dr. John Posey.

Prairie du chien
Decr 12, 1827.

Dear Brother,

I am yet ignorant of the welfare of my family, and friends, in your quarter. I have neither recd. a line, or heard one word from a passing stranger from home, since we parted at the Saline. This deathlike silence is extremely painful to me in my seeming banishment. To be seperated from my family so long is of itself sufficiently disagreeable; but to be cut off from all knowledge of them is distressing. No regular mail comes here, and the mail goes by chance oppertunities, till there is postage enough collected to send a special messenger, and then the money is thus applied.

My health continues good, and were my mind at ease in relation to my family, I should be in tolerable spirits. Sometimes a fit of thinking, and mental pain in regard to my family, causes some head ache. Otherwise I have not had a days sickness since we parted.[22]

For many women on the Wisconsin frontier, the domestic duties expected of them—keeping an orderly home, bearing and raising children, cooking, sewing, and washing clothes, among other tasks—required long hours of isolated drudgery. Rural Wisconsin lacked some of the close community ties that bound women together in more settled regions of the United States. This separation from the close-knit world of family and friends often exacted a heavy toll on the women of early Wisconsin, as seen in the following letter most likely written by Elizabeth Thérèse Baird (1810–1890).

Born in Prairie du Chien with the last name Fisher, Elizabeth was the daughter of a British fur trader and a mother of mixed French and Native descent. She married Henry S. Baird, a promising attorney, when she was only fourteen years old, and the couple settled in Green Bay. A talented woman with knowledge of the fur trade and with contacts in the American Indian community, the young Elizabeth Baird found the early years of her marriage difficult. Years later, she recalled, "As I did not talk English, speaking only a few words, and understanding it as little, conversation with my neighbors was not interesting to me, and I did not seek them as I would have done had they spoken French. In consequence, my life was very solitary. My

Elizabeth Thérèse Baird, ca. 1879. WHI IMAGE ID 5210

husband would mount his horse directly after breakfast, and I would not see him again until near evening. . . . That I shed many tears I cannot deny."[23]

This letter—believed to be from Elizabeth to Frances and Hannah Irwin, as the letter is signed E.T.B. and Baird was a frequent guest of the Irwins—illustrates how dramatic the physical separation from friends and family could be.

[1836]

My Dear *Sisters* Hannah & Frank,

I should have gone up to spend the day with you to-day, but I would have no way to come home if I did ride upon the lumber waggon with Thomas, he is going to the farm for potatoes. I wish you would write me a long *letter* by his return.

I send you two shirts of Mrs. Hart's for the society, you will oblige me very much if you can do them this week. I will not ask you to sew for next week. You cannot imagin how very lonely I feel. I am now at liberty to give way to my feelings. Lib is as happy as the day is long, but all that only increases my—what—would you believe it if I said I was low spirited, I do not think you would. Well, I was *sick* yesterday, and I felt as if I would give any thing to see you both. I want to see you so today, that I do not know what to do. I think if I could see any *thing* or any *body* in the *shape* of a [blank space]. I do not care what, I would ask *it* or *him* or *she* or whatever it might happen to be, to take me up to see you; I wish something would come along here. I would not care if it should be a *cow* or a good sized *hog* (for I would have pity on a small one; for I have you know that I have not quite lost all the feeling I ever had.) I think if I was so fortunate as to meet with either of the about mentioned *Cretars* [Creatures], I would be apt to strad[d]le one & make my appearance up to your happy dwelling—

I know you will feel sorry to hear. I am in such low spirits as this *scrawl* will lead you to beleive. but so it is, and I cannot help it, the best way I can *fix* it, Lib says that by this, she would judge that I had the *blues* most *horribly* what do you think? I think that I am so blue that I am almost black, but that is no news to you, but as I am very *economical*. I do not lik[e] to waist paper by let[t]ing it go up to you blank—I think I hear you say; "foolish child why do you not save your time instead of your paper, it is more *precious*.["] If I was by you I would thank you for all you would say: so upon reflection I will close this *string* of *nonsense*, save my *time* save my *credit*, if any I have; and let my paper go. Now good bye & be I beg of you both "charitable" to your

Sincere but Crazy Friend
E T B[24]

Another example of the heavy toll that separation from one's hometown and family could exact comes from the pen of Racheline S. Wood Bass. Racheline was twenty-eight years old when she wrote the following two letters and had moved from Enosburgh, Vermont, to Platteville in southeastern Wisconsin during the late 1830s. Although she married James W. Bass, a Platteville merchant, shortly after writing the first of these two letters, she still deeply missed her relatives back in Vermont. In these letters, Racheline attempts to convince her sister, Mary Wood, to move to Wisconsin. She uses a blend of persuasion, admonishment, guilt, and anger to express her feelings of loneliness and homesickness in a land far away from kin. In addition, she shares the frustrations and joys she has experienced teaching school. Part of the manuscript is torn and missing. Where conjectural readings could be made from context, they have been inserted in braces—e.g., {yet still}. Where too much text was lost to make a conjecture, the words "page torn" have been inserted in brackets.

Plattville
March 10th 1840

No one even if sis M is not in town must read this. I am well much love to you all. Send this directly to M. now be honest.

Dear Sis M.

I had not designed to write you untill I had received an answer to my last, (which by the way is a long time in arriving.) It is now 8 o'clock and first the mail leaves at 10 of necessity I must be brief. Well M, I am now sitting at the fireside of a particular friend, vis. Mrs. Kendals and what do you think I have to say to you this, charming spring, morn. I will try to tell you though I am well aware that I expose myself to you severe thoughts and censures. My first object is to give you an invitation to come to this far West; the country which I have chosen for my future home, provided Providence favors my present arrangements. I have been earnestly solicited to commence a select school for girls or Misses this spring, and had thought of doing so but have now decided to give up that employment and now if you were but here you could have the situation, which would [be] a very pleasant and lucrative one. I had limited my number to 30 should have had four dollars per quarter. Do you not wish you were here. I do. You cannot possibly be here before some time in May when the school will be perhaps taken up, but there are many vacancies in the Territory; I have no doubt you can be profitably employed as a teacher within a short [time] and perhaps immediately in P[latteville]. You will pardon me when I tell you that I expect to have a home of my own in a short time, that is, in some two or three months and shall be happy to have you share it with me. About a year since I became acquainted with a Mr. Bass formerly from Braintree Vermont and who is now a merchant in this pleasant vilage, a strictly moral person, a member of the total abstinance society and is reputed to be worth with his partner, who is his cousin, some thousands exclusive of all debts. I think it more than probable you will not like him but if I do no matter for your opinion. I have frequently spoken to him of you, he urges me to write for you, says he will share his loaf etc with you in which I know he is sincere. I am ashamed of what I have writen but you are my sister; no other one recieves this confidence; how much I now need a mothers and sisters advice. You wish to know how you will get here you must not come alone. A Mr Fidder in Braintree, a law[y]er, an intimate acquaintance of Mr Bass, with his wife and child expect to be here in May. Mr. B will write him respecting taking you with them. The time before he starts is so limited that I hardly know what directions to give you. Mr F. will be requested to write you directions which you, or you can get father to answer. You must of course expedite business. You must not start with less than $100 though you will not probably spend that sum unless adverse fortune attend you. Do not let the above sum discourage you, for I presume you will not expend more than half of it and you can earn money three times as fast here as there; and I believe you will enjoy better health. We have good society beter than any other place in the mining section of the country. Do not attribute what I have written above to improper motives, for I should not and had not designed to write you a word of the above subject untill some time hence had I not been advised to it and had not hoped the vacancy in school would not be filled untill your arrival. Come, Come! get a good supply of clothes any good ones too. Take as much money as you please you can get good interest and please take up my note and bring {that} amount along with you. You should purchase a large [page torn] traveling trunk that with your large one if you {yet still} have it will I think contain some of my bed things and sustain my share of the expence. Perhaps Mother will take my bed and throw in some flannel or some other articles which may be servicable to me. Do as you please about the last. Do not take other luggage than the above with the exception of a carpet bag which you will find very convenient. Take some pains at large places to get some patterns or at least to notice about them. Carry your money about your person and be very discreet in your conduct; these cautions I suppose are unneces[sary] but experience is a good teacher. If I knew that you would come I would direct you to get me a dossen of good used silver teaspoons, 3 large ones 2 desert ones 1 salt one, a pair of sugar tongs a cream spoon with part of my money. I have two hundred dollars which I have earned within a few months to help myself with.

Mr Dixon on account of ill health is obliged to relinquish the school here his place will be soon supplied. We had an interesting examination. Would you not liked to have been present and to have seen me paraded before a meetinghouse full of spectators. It was said that I played my part creditably. I would not supposed that I could have mustered as much confidence as I really did on the occ[asio]n. If you write to Mr F. direct to I. P. Fidder Esq Braintree Vermont. Much love to all the family and to sister & to uncle F's family. . . .

Racheline S. Wood

[P.S.] If you should not come with Mr F. improve the first suitable opportunity as probably there will be many for I do indeed think it best that you come here. You shall not want for a home. I would like to have you live constantly with me so no matter for schools

Platteville

May 3d 1840

Dear sister M.

I recieved your expected letter of the 28th ultimo [i.e., last month], and I will not say that its contents were as acceptable as I had anticipated. After I wrote you, untill I recieved yours, I had anticipated so much your coming, and the pleasure of a sisters society, that I had wrought myself into the belief that you would surely come to this pleasant country. But I was destined to disappointment I was strongly tempted [to] be angry with your little resolution for I ascribed your decision, either to lack of that trait of character or, to indifference to a sister. Reflect on the subject a moment and you will accede to my opinion. Remember that I am far from the land of my birth without a relative, (one excepted) while you are surrounded by friends known from childhood and yet you, after, expression some two or three times a desire to become acquainted with and to visit this country when a good opportunity perhaps is better than you will again have, fail in coming. I will endeavour not to censure friends for discouraging your coming. You speak of the giant distance. It is no farther than it was two years ago and I scanned it and never have regretted the attempt. You say you would come among entire strangers. Is your sister a stranger? When I came did I find relatives a brother and a sister? Your time is so limited that you cannot get in readiness for the journey. We are no such wonderfull people that you need let such a favourable opportunity pass unimproved on that account. Your reasons I considered as null and void. One word more, we do not wish you to come without you are willing to make some little present sacrifice, to get here for if you are not we should fear your would not be contented when here. I have to-day had a little cry on the above account. Mr B seemed much disappointed at your decision. He had been at the trouble to write very particularly to Mr Fidder at Braintree respecting your accompan[y]ing him and family. Be not angry for I pardon you all. If you do not wish to come sure I ought not to be selfish about it. . . .

A young man in order to resist the multitude of constant tempta[tion] which almost inevitably lead to ruin must necessarily possess the sternest determination to resist every temptation, to avoid the numerous snares which would lure him from the path of virtue and safety. I am now referring particularly of this western region for every days observation demonstrates the above assertion. I many times almost decide to invite some of my eastern acquaintance to come this way but have never done it. Though we have among our citizens many of the most refined intelligent people yet the whole mining country abounds with the dregs of society. You would perhaps infer, from the above, that I am getting wearied with this western country but indeed I am not, I like it as well as ever. Platteville is a most delightful town (not a township) a mile square containing some 150 dwelling houses, many of them of the snuggest neatest kind; not large and airy like those in countrys covered with stumps stones and forests, yet answering every purpose, and now while vegetation is rapidly advancing the offering of nature is most lovely, the prospect is most charming. I suppose and am told by settlers there is no one inland town in this Territory of the age of Platteville, that is as promising or as fair to become a place of consequence; its mining and farming resources are almost unrivaled. But pardon me. I had forgotten to whom I was writing. What do you care for this distant region but it is my home & I am interested

May 17th. Mr. Bass has gone to Racine a flourishing town on the lake Michigan 160 miles distant on business. (He by the way owns between 3 and 400 acres of land near there which he considers very valuable) and I am so lonely; indeed I have been almost inclined to be homesick for a day or two first. Oh! How I long to fold those *dear, very dear* cousins and sisters to my heart. Sometimes I feel as though I *could not* be denied. People sometimes tell me that I have a hard heart that I cannot love like others but they know me not I do not expect that Mr B will return under 4 or 5 days. He left last Tuesday. M you may now call him brother, as he became on the 16th ult. I suppose Marietta received a paper conveying that intelligence. Dear sis my home is in this distant land and you hard hearted one why delay to make it (at least) for a while yours likewise

Yet I am contented though I would be much more so had I my dear sis, and the smiles of my saviour with me I live at such a poor dying rate so far from God that I fear I shall come short of heaven. Dear sister do not I intreat you do not forget me, and your brother, who is without the one thing needful, in your love. Mr B.s parents and sisters are most of them professors of religion; his mother letters breathe a most christian spirit. As a sister you would like to know somewhat of my temporal prospects. I wrote my last in such haste that I have no distinct recollection of what I did write. Our last school session closed the 14th Feb. I had not had a weeks [page torn] in ten months, had earned in that time about $250. You cannot well imagine {my} joy, almost unbounded, which I experienced the succeeding day. I felt as though my shaccles were off; as though I was free as a bird in air, I was not required to be in school the next day, the next week or month. Notwithstanding, I do love schoolkeeping, and, many times, when I now see my dear pupils assembling at the entering hour and place, I almost wish that I was going too. I love my dear schollars and they seem to reciprocate that feeling. But I forget my subject. I think that in my last I mentioned that Mr B engaged in the Mercantile business, he is, a partner with his cousin I Wales Bass are, carrying on an extensive business. Since last Nov Mr B says they have sold abbout 11,000 dollars worth of goods, mostly for cash down. They own a good store some valuable farm lots a barn, domestic animals etc etc We are now boarding, but expect to commence keeping house soon which I am in great haste to do, though I much dread the extreme warm weather. You will I think by this time expect that you will not see me in June. No we cannot come, and more I know not when that happy time will arrive. Had I wings with swiftest speed would they bear me east where my dear friends my kindred dwell. I fear sometimes that I shall never see you all again but I always banish those unwelcome fears. Do not fear for my temporal welfare I have every necessary comfort of life . . .

Your ever affectionate sister

R.S.W. Bass[25]

Dedication and perseverance were characteristics expected of missionaries, but even the most strong-hearted Christian often missed the comforts of home when proselytizing in American Indian communities. Florantha Thompson Sproat (1811–1883) was born in Middleborough, Massachusetts, and married Presbyterian minister Granville Sproat in 1838. Shortly after their marriage, the couple moved to the Ojibwe mission at La Pointe on Madeline Island in Lake Superior. In this series of letters to her family in Massachusetts, Florantha describes the life of a female missionary in northern Wisconsin. Her letters mix the humorous, the mundane, and the tragic, all while conveying her feelings of detachment from ordinary family life.

June 23, 1839.

My dear Mother,

Your letter I can assure you was joyfully received, a week since. In it I found many interesting items concerning friends. When I received your letter I was just recovering from confinement, am now quite well but without my natural strength. You alone of all my friends can sympathize with me when I tell you that on the morning of May 16th I gave birth to a lovely little daughter, but God took its spirit to himself. It was perfect in form—a full grown child—but still-born. Had there been a skillful physician at hand, in an unnatural birth, they might have saved our child. After prayer had been offered a hymn sung our babe was followed by husband, Mr. Hall, Dr. Borup, Mr. Baraga the catholic priest and a concourse of weeping natives to a resting place on the shore of Lake Superior beneath tall trees. The event being so uncommon here it excited much feeling among the indians. I had made too much dependance, and my affections too much centered in my child. Even now, tho I know it is for the best, my heart hungers for my babe.

We have had rather of a still winter there being no indians, but our own band, near us. But this place is fast filling with indians from the interior for there is to be held a treaty with them for land. Heathenism and depravity we see on every hand, but the indians are not so far sunk in depravity as many of other nations, from the accounts of the missionaries. With regard to the prosperity of our missionary efforts I hardly know how to write. To persons with the sanguine belief that the only obstacle in the way of christianizing the indians is their lack of knowledge of gospel truth, and that we have only need to point them the way to Heaven and they will walk in it, would find themselves sadly disappointed. For the human heart is the same here as in our favored and enlightened land, where many will pass their lives unconverted beneath the full blaze of Gospel light. . . . At such times I think of home and how pleased friends would be to witness such customs. Tell Julius that when I saw the dog trains pass I thought what pleasure he would take in going with them if he were here. And indeed they are the most laughable curiosities I have witnessed since I have been in the country. To see two or three half-sized dogs, sometimes in tandom, sometimes abreast, conveying at full speed, two or three full-sized grown people must look laughable to anyone. I can think of nothing else but

Cinderella's pumpkin coach and mice. I have been on a dog train two or three times. One I will describe, it being a laughable event. We have two large dogs, the fleetest and strongest of any in the place. One morning the last of winter Mr. Hall said he was going to the Fort, and if I wished to have a ride I might go with him. I gladly accepted and got into the little carriage made for the purpose. Before Mr. Hall could get in the dogs set off at their greatest speed, delighted with the fun. Mr. Hall made greatest effort to overtake me, but he might as well have tried to overtake a wild

Florantha Thompson Sproat in a portrait painted by her father, Cephas Thompson, in 1838. WHI IMAGE ID 2938

deer in the forest, and I was hurried at greatest speed over the plain and through the forest, until in passing a log house my fleet horses happened to spy a friend of their own species—or rather, I might judge, an enemy— they made a sudden turn, jumped over a woodpile, and seized him by the throat. Then would have ensued a bloody battle had not some men come to my assistance, and guided the team to their destination. Not feeling any danger I was pleased with my ride, excited with laughter, while those that we passed looked on in astonishment. . . .

Yours affectionately

Florantha T. Sproat

Mar. 23. [1842]

Last night Mrs. Wheeler gave birth to a dead child. She had been con-fined to her bed for two months previously, on account of convulsions and other difficulties. Again I must speak of the great necessity for women missionaries to this country, to be of good and firm health. None should come but of strong and rugged constitution if they wish to be of use. . . .

Tonight I went to our fish barrel for some fish for supper and found it all spoiled. Upon telling husband he said, "What shall we eat?" I said "We've nothing but pork," and he "I cannot eat pork"—but we had some warm potatoes and cold pork and beans—the remains of yesterday when we had company—Mrs. Bushnell and Miss Spooner—to tea. And I had some cake made from risen dough and maple sugar. It was light, I assure you, but I must add that the supper made some of us sick.

Mar. 25 [1842]

A beautiful evening although it was a stormy morning which prevented me from washing, so I have been doing a little of many things, and sitting with Mrs. Wheeler. The Indians have all gone to their sugar-making, so we have less company. I am sitting in my little bed-room, writing this on my toilette made of a packing box. Sarah Hall is rolling and tumbling over my bed and Margaret sitting in the dining room stringing rags for a rug. And now my dear friends I would like to know what you are doing, how I wish that I could see you all once more. I am more at leisure than I have been since I have been here. I teach a class of indian women for awhile in the evenings. this stopped on their going to make sugar.

Mar. 26. [1842]

This day has been a splendid one. this morning we—husband, Margaret, and myself—commenced doing a large washing. We had just begun when Dr. Borup with his wife and family came and asked me to take a ride, so I hurried and got one boiler of clothes on, left Margaret in charge to keep them boiling, while Miss Spooner and I put on our black hoods and cloaks and got into the sleigh. Dr. drove us back and forth upon the lake, which was quite refreshing, home again I finished the washing, have gotten & finished our supper and now I am trying to write with Sarah Hall witching about. I have had so much charge of her she is as much at home with me as with her mother. . . .

April 2 [1842]

Our expectations have been raised this morning for a smoke signal announced that there is an arrival. When persons arrive at this place in the winter they come to the shore opposite and there make a smoke signal. Those who see it first go with canoe and bring them over. At this time we are in expectation of men that were sent for the mail, and are in hopes the smoke signals their arrival. You have no idea of our feelings at such a time. One fact I would mention—that all letters that you receive from us, fall, winter or spring are carried by men 4 or 5 hundred miles through a thick and uninhabitable wilderness with snow 4 or 5 feet deep. They go thus far before they reach any sign of habitation. They then leave the mail and return with one for this place. I hope, at this time, I shall not be disappointed by not receiving letters from you.

The mail has arrived being many [letters] for others and none for me. My disappointment is great. You dwelling in the midst of friends and comforts remember but faintly your far-off missionary daughter & sister, and she never ceases to remember you with love and tenderness. I had expected that this mail would bring a letter relative to my going home and now I must give up the fond hope of seeing you as I would not go without hearing from you first. . . .

F. Sproat

Oct. 10, 1842.

My dear mother

It was with mingled pleasure and pain that we received the box from home, and opened it on the day before yesterday. The portrait of our mother was received by us with high pleasure and delight, it was very natural, and for which father has our sincere thanks and gratitude. When I came to look for letters and tokens of remembrances from home and finding only yours and Elviras containing only a few lines, and no news, I felt pained and disappointed for I had been waiting with fond hopes of great pleasure half the year, not hearing from home the time. The bedquilt gave me much pleasure. I have been looking over the squares seeing the names of different friends who are dear. give my love and thanks to them all. The articles of the box are very useful for our mission and its opperations, for which your mission has our thanks. You ask what you shall make for the coming year. I think if you will make small quilts for cradles and one or two for cribs they would be useful (I may want one myself) & quilted skirts of dark cambrick. I need one very much, they are a good thing for this country, and are never sent to us. If you could sent a pattern unmade of dark calico—I like your taste—for a dress it would be very acceptable, or pieces or remnants of any kind of calico, two or three yard pieces of fine print would be very useful. I write this to let you know what *would* be useful. I have often wished for coarse earthenware pudding dishes and plates of which we have none in this part of the country. they would be more serviceable to me than most anything else. they could come safely packed with the clothes. I wish you would without fail send your box to Boston by the last of March or first of May as Mr. G. sends goods about that time, if not it will be uncertain about our getting it the same season. Childrens colored stockings and childrens clothes of all kinds, are needed. Those little frocks fit Sarah H. prettily. Best love to all friends. tell Elvira that I have written to herself, Olivia Juliet and Mrs. King without having received an answer. write oftener. a long letter.

F. Sproat

[P.S.] I wish you would send some fall crookneck squash seeds and some cranberry beans and some of those early tender beans the pods round, and other kinds of early summer squash seeds. You see I have written somewhat of a begging letter. I mean if you can. We never get those things.[26]

While some women settlers felt neglected by their families in distant locales, others were abandoned by their husbands and found themselves without financial support. Sarah Sheesuck Leach (1809–1884) was a member of the Brothertown nation of Indians who had emigrated from New York to Wisconsin in the 1830s and received a reservation from the federal government. In 1839, the Brothertown were granted citizenship by Congress. The reservation was abolished, and the tribe divided the land into sixty-acre parcels among tribal members. Under Wisconsin law, a woman's property was transferred to her husband upon marriage, but the Brothertown granted women—married, unmarried, and widowed—the same property rights as men. The tribe, however, excluded women who married outside the tribe. Because Leach had married a white man, she lost her right to the allotted land. After her husband left her without any financial support and without land, Leach petitioned the Wisconsin legislature for a divorce, rather than go through the more time-consuming court process. The legislature denied her request. Sarah Leach died in the town of Brothertown, and her 1884 obituary described her as a "kind friend, accommodating neighbor and a good citizen."[27] The following document is Leach's impassioned petition to the Wisconsin legislature.

To the Council and House of Representatives of the Territory of Wisconsin. [Submitted, January 14, 1842]

This the petition of your peti[ti]oner Sarah Leach would respectfully represent to your honorable body that in the year 1837 your petitioner was legally married to John Leach a non-commissioned officer in the United States Army and that she resided with him a ~~short~~ time at Green Bay Wisconsin Territory, the marriage having taken place on the 4th June 1837 and her husband John Leach having left that place on the 16th or 17th of the same month: since which time your peti[ti]oner has not seen her husband John Leach although she has constantly resided at or near Green Bay Wisconsin Territory.

That at the departure of said John Leach from Green Bay he made no provision for the support of your petitioner, but that for the last four years she has been obliged to provide for herself by the labour of her own hands.

That owing to her marriage with said Leach she was deprived of all right and share in the land or property of the Brothertown Nation of Indians to which she belonged. That your petitioner has conclusive evidence that her husband has abandonned her permanently; Your petitioner having received a letter within a short time from said Leach stating that he never intends to live with your petitioner again nor in any manner conduce to her support. Your petitioner therefore prays your honorable body to make such legal provision for your petitioner's being divorced from said John Leach as it may appear proper to the wisdom of your honorable body. Your petitioner would in the difficulty of procuring documentary proofs of the injurious treatment and desertion she has experienced beg leave to refer to the Honorable Charles C. P. Arndt of the Council or to Mr. J. G. Knapp now at Madison. And your petitioner will ever pray.

Sarah Leach[28]

Settlers who traveled from Europe were also separated from family and friends, but their experience in Wisconsin entailed the added difficulty of adapting to entirely different social customs, foods, languages, and laws. Although many immigrants considered the benefits of their new lives in Wisconsin to outweigh the drawbacks, some early arrivals were frustrated by their American circumstances. Jon N. Bjørndalen wrote the following letter to his parents in Norway in 1844, and it was later published in the Norwegian newspaper *Morgenbladet*. He is an excellent example of someone who found himself disenchanted with the land of opportunity. The letter was originally written in Norwegian.

Milwaukee County
January 5, 1844

I write you briefly for your information, because several of my countrymen are planning to go to America. I hope that they will not disregard my humble communication.

I think of my countrymen with tender feelings and remember how they imagine that as soon as they get to America, great glories will open up to them. And how could they believe otherwise, for almost all reports and letters received in Norway from America were good. But this is very wrong; only about a third part of these letters is true. People only write down accounts of the good, although they themselves have had no experience of it. As we traveled up through the country we all had high hopes that we should be happy, but these were disappointed. The first thing we encountered on our arrival in Milwaukee was two of our countrymen down at the wharf. Not until then did we see the good things one acquires in this country—an emaciated body and a sallow face! This is how almost all our immigrants look. The ague and other pestilential fevers were widespread so that one victim could not help the other. All who have this illness become weak, are never safe from it, and daily suffer from poor health. The heavy air is depressing, and people walk around bowed like slaves weighed down by their chains and deprived of their freedom. In the summer the climate is far too hot; during the daytime the heat is so severe that when you work sweat pours out all over your body, as if you had been drenched by rain, and during the night everything is covered by a poisonous fog.

There are a lot of snakes here, five or six different kinds, most of which are unfamiliar to me. They even get into the houses; rattlesnakes, for instance, have often been found on the floor. They are able to burrow down into the ground and thus get into people's houses. The biggest I have seen are as thick as a man's arm. In the short time I have been here I have killed many of them.

The land the Norwegians have settled consists mostly of woods and swamps, of which there are a countless number. They are used for grazing because the woodland hardly affords good grazing as it is so extensively covered with oak bushes and hazel bushes. It looks like land thickly covered with juniper and other small trees. It would be difficult to clear this land because of the big knolls and the roots the bushes put out, and the oak trees are as heavy to clear away as stones. The settlers do not get much milk from the cattle fed with swamp grass in winter unless they add to it kohlrabies, potatoes, and Indian corn.

You have probably heard how light the taxes are said to be here; and it is true enough that the first two or three years the tax on eighty acres of land is only $1. But later a man goes around and puts a tax on your land, on what you have fenced in, on the land you have cleared; if you have built a house, you have to pay tax on that; you have to pay tax on the cattle, on a cart, on a house covered with boards; in short, you have to pay taxes on everything you own. And the value of everything is assessed by the men who travel around and inspect it all. Thus it is estimated that when a Norwegian has lived here long enough to have his road all made and his house and farming tools in good condition, he will have to pay from $10 to $16; that is, $1 out of every $100, to the government. If a man has lent money, he is taxed 1 per cent, so that, in fact, he almost has to pay for his own harvest and work.

I shall have to tell you also about the Mormon religion, which is the most miserable sect you can imagine. The first one to adopt this detestable religion was Ole Olsen Sandvigen. Now he has lured several of his countrymen into this abominable kind of worship, for instance, two of the sons of Lars Folseland and Anne Christiansdatter. There is a whole sect of them in Illinois, where Ole Sandvigen is staying. If he makes more visits to the Norwegian settlement, probably many will be converted. I do not understand this religion, and I do not want to understand it. They believe that their baptism is the gate to heaven, and that it is easy to go there once you have been baptized. They believe that they can cure the sick, even that they can help those of the dead who in their opinion have not been saved to enter heaven by means of their baptism. There are many Anabaptists, but none are so ridiculous and detestable as the Mormons.

Daily wages are much lower now than they used to be. Money is scarce, and you can get practically nothing but trade in kind unless you know the language and travel to distant markets. I do not deny that if one has good health and a happy disposition, in time it will be easier to make a living. But when the Norwegians have to work for Americans, they are at first much too weak to stand their work. You work strenuously from morning till noon without rest. Then when you have gobbled down your food, you have to start work again. I am reminded of the rush in Norway when we tried to save the dry hay from the rain!

Thus, I do not advise any of my relatives to come to America. If you could see the conditions of the Norwegians in America at present, you would certainly be frightened; illness and misery are so prevalent that many have died. One cannot imagine anything more misleading than the tempting and deceptive letters that reach Norway, for these letters have not only taken away people's relatives, but they have almost taken away their lives. One might suppose that the emigrants believe that they are well off, but this is far from true. Except for a few men, all are in misery from illness, starvation, and cold. Most of them lack money and are unable to work—certainly the greatest misery anyone can imagine. I want to tell you briefly how many of those who emigrated from Tind have died: Knud Mærum and his insane son Thore, Tosten Mærum and his wife, Jacob Ejhoug, Ingebret Berge and his wife, Ole Sanden, Osten Eggerud and his wife, Gro Eggerud, Sigurd Vemork, Anne Halvorsdatter Laavekaase, Anne Boen, and besides many small children, Halvor Jorrisdahl and Gunner from Sjotvedt; all told sixty-eight grown people and children.

Both my wife and I have been ill with the ague from eight days before Holy-Cross Day to Christmas; but since we feel a little better now, we hope that God will let us live and that in time we shall get our health back. But even if we do get better, we shall have to keep quiet and not try to work for the rest of the winter. So far we have a debt of 16 specie dollars [i.e., gold or silver], and we are staying with the Holje Grimsruds, who are good, congenial people. Time is heavy on our hands, and we are not happy in our emigration. If the Almighty grants us good health and we can make enough money, our greatest wish is to go back to old Norway. When you have neither health nor any pleasures here in America, it is better to live in your native country even if you own nothing. America will always be unhealthful, and no Norseman is ever going to be happy here.

Many persons here in America have behaved very badly, for instance, Knud Svalestuen, who lured so many people out to great misery. The statement in his letter that he was the owner of a great deal of land was the greatest falsehood you can imagine, for he did not own a thing here in America. In the same way, Jan Knudsen Traen inveigled his brothers out to great misery. He promised them that if they would pay the passage for Ole Sanden, he would pay them back when they arrived, but he did not even own the clothes he was wearing or enough food to give them a meal. His sister now lives on charity, for she is unable to provide for her small children. Likewise Jon Nielsen Rue with his deceitful letters so shamefully induced his parents to come here to utter wretchedness. And there are many other such swindlers.

The Norwegians have a good pastor—a Dane—and they have sermons every Sunday. Children are taught both in the Norwegian and the English school and, with God's help, will be encouraged in their Christian religion.

In conclusion, then, my relatives, do not think of coming to America at all. Dear parent and brothers and sisters, and you my dear Halvor Gjosdal, do not let America enter your thoughts any more. And I do not advise Gro and Gunnild to follow me but to stay in their native country. Time is short, and I shall now stop though I have much more to write about. I send my best greetings and may the spirit of truth be in your hearts and aid you in your several undertakings.[29]

Ole Munch Ræder (1815–1895), a Norwegian legal scholar, was sent by his government to study the American legal system in 1847 and 1848. He visited Wisconsin in the summer and fall of 1847. His letters describing the Norwegian community during his American tour were reprinted in newspapers in Norway and offered those back home another glimpse of life in America. In this excerpt from one of his letters that appeared in the Norwegian newspaper *Den Norske Rigstidende* in November 1847, Ræder recounts some complaints from dissatisfied Norwegian settlers, but offers a more balanced view of Wisconsin than Bjørndalen. The letter was originally written in Norwegian.

I must add that, among all the people I have talked with—and they are not a few—I have found very few who said they were dissatisfied and wanted to return to Norway, and with some of these it was more a matter of talk than of a real desire to go. One man said he wanted to return home because his wife did not like it here; another, who said he was a Quaker, was dissatisfied with the schools. Both of them had been talking in this vein for a long time, without making any real move in that direction but rather the opposite. A little merchant from Drammen, on the other hand, seemed to mean it seriously; he has been rather unfortunate, for which I am sorry, as he seems to be a very fine man. And it is not strange if there are some who have been ruined through their emigration. The emigration fever spread through our country districts like a disease, paying no heed to age or sex, rich or poor, the diligent worker or the lazy good-for-nothing. Naturally, many have emigrated who are totally unfit for the strenuous life here, which demands so much energy, common sense, and endurance if one is to succeed. It is equally true that many have made a mistake in buying

MADISON IN JUNE 1837.

Lithograph made from an 1837 painting of the Peck cabin, the first settlers' home in Madison. WHI IMAGE ID 3804

or claiming land before they had either the necessary understanding or means to proceed with its cultivation. The fact that there have not been more wrecks than there have, in view of all the mistakes made, gives evidence both of the inherent strength of character of our people and of the excellence of the country itself.

I do not mean to imply that few complaints are heard. Quite the contrary. In addition to the fact that many, indeed most, admit that they had expected the land to be far better than it actually proved to be and that they had been fooled, to some extent, by the false reports contained in letters, there are many other complaints; but all of them are of such a nature that time and habit will presumably remedy the situation. Some complain that the work is too strenuous, others that there is so much ungodliness, others that there is too much sickness. One woman complained that there seemed to be less real nourishment in the food here than in Norway; no matter how much good food she gave her husband, he simply would not gain in weight. Possibly, she thought, and very likely with good reason, this was due to the severe heat which, coupled with strenuous labor, sapped his energy.

. . . Still it is a fact that many people have suffered much from these fevers, especially the immigrants. Last fall was particularly bad in this respect, as the heat had been oppressive. This year the situation is not quite so bad. I have been in the best of health, with the exception of a few days, in spite of the abrupt changes from hot to cold weather which we have had and which are said to have been particularly severe this year. Many complain of the sudden change from the severely cold winter to the hot summer, a condition which is said to prevail in most parts of America; for example, in New York the winter is said to be as cold as in Christiania [i.e., modern Oslo] and the summer as hot as in Naples; I do not know how much truth there is in that.

Some complain that the thunderstorms and other natural phenomena here are so violent that the uninitiated become thoroughly alarmed. A Norwegian family found it so terrifying at first to see "the heavens in a blaze" that they crept into a cellar. It is true that the thunder rumbles with great majesty here and that the lightning flashes across the heavens in a particularly lively fashion, when a storm is given free rein, and that happens often.

The worst complaint of all is homesickness; everyone experiences that, of course. But time can heal even deeper wounds than that of having been severed from one's native land. Furthermore, most of the immigrants seem to cherish more or less consciously a hope of returning some day to their native land, having realized only after they had broken away how strong were the ties that held them there. . . .

You will probably ask if I found anything that would indicate that dissatisfaction with political conditions in Norway had influenced anyone to emigrate; in Norway, as you know, there has been considerable loose talk to this effect. Of course I could not very well ask people bluntly for fear that they might suspect me of being some sort of inquisitor. Nevertheless I gave them all an opportunity to express themselves on this question by asking them their motives for emigrating. All except one, who said he had religious grounds, spoke of economic motives, of the hope that their children would have a better future here, and so forth. Only two people remarked casually that people in Norway did not enjoy so great a degree of freedom. I asked one of them if he did not think that the people are their own masters and lawmakers in Norway also, but he answered that this was only on paper. "A person there isn't even master of his own body"—which, however, could as well be said of people here in America. The same man expressed his satisfaction with economic conditions, by saying, "Here even a tramp can enjoy a chicken dinner once in a while."[30]

> Although all new settlers from overseas experienced difficulties in adapting to their new home, many felt that the new opportunities Wisconsin provided far outweighed the hardships of frontier life. Edwin and Martha Bottomley related their opinions about moving to Wisconsin in a letter to their family in England. (For background on the Bottomleys, see pages 53–54.) Even though the change of surroundings would ultimately prove fatal to Edwin three years later, the couple's letter reflects the strong conviction that many immigrants held concerning the future of their families in America. As with the Bottomleys' previous letters, the spelling has been silently corrected and the first word of each sentence has been capitalized.

Rochester

March 17th 1847

Dear Father:

. . . I shall now proceed to notice a few remarks in your letter which a note of mine caused you to make. Now Dear father when I said that I Should be under the necessity of refusing your request if you Desired me to come back to England I did not mean that I had no Desire to see you all and if I was to say so I Should not speak the truth for I often think of you all and It would be a happy Day to me to once more behold you all again but whether Such will ever be my lot or not To see you all again in this world is only known to god but if it be [h]is will that we must not meet on earth again I hope and trust that we shall meet in heaven.

Dear father you know what a fathers Love is for his children both when he Dandles them on his knee and when they are gone from his own fire side to struggle with the world for their Daily bread so that you can judge of my situation as well if not better than I can myself. These Little ones look to me for bread yet and my object in coming to this country was to enable me to procure them this and although we have been Disappointed in our crops and afflicted with Sickness I have not [the] least fear but I Shall have sufficient for them and I believe when they have to struggle for themselves they will be better able to Do it in this country than in England. . . .

your affectionate Son and Daughter

Edwin & Martha Bottomley[31]

Because acclimation to American life was difficult for new arrivals, families often sent one member overseas first in order to scout the territory—thus smoothing the process of adjustment for the rest of the family. Twenty-five-year-old John Kerler Jr. (1823–1885) left Bavaria in 1848 at the request of his father, John Kerler Sr. The elder Kerler wished to leave the turmoil created by revolution in Germany, and the younger Kerler's mission was to locate a place to which the remaining family could emigrate. In the summer of 1849, the rest of the Kerler family arrived in Milwaukee and purchased farmland in nearby Greenfield, which became a thriving farm community by 1850 with half its residents of German descent. In this letter to his friend August Frank (who would later become his brother-in-law), John Kerler Jr. relates some of the more important adjustments that German migrants often made when moving to the United States. Kerler later moved west and worked as an Indian trader in Minnesota, the Dakotas, Montana, Alberta, and Manitoba. The letter was originally written in German.

Milwaukee

March 27. [1850]

My dear Mr. Frank:

. . . A main point to consider is the language. Since English is spoken in court, trading, and in general (you find this all over North America) it is a little hard at first. Milwaukee is the only place in which I found that the Americans concern themselves with learning German, and where the German language and German ways are bold enough to take a foothold. You will find inns, beer cellars and billiard and bowling alleys, as well as German beer, something you do not find much of in this country. The Dutchman (the Americans call the Germans this name by way of derision) plays a more independent role—has balls, concerts and theaters—

naturally not to be compared to those in Germany and has even managed to get laws printed in German. His vote carries a heavy weight at election time. You will find no other place in which so much has been given the Germans, and if you value *this*, you may safely prefer Wisconsin, and especially Milwaukee, to other places. . . .

Now, my dear Mr. Frank, you have a long epistle about "do this and that," and even though written hastily, I think you should be able to get a picture of the conditions and the possibilities of relief when traveling. There is much and also little to say about America itself. You have freedom, you have income, you have the sky and the earth, but also a strange language, many low-class and rough country people, and little of the enjoyment that could so easily be provided in social and other ways. This we miss doubly here because, in addition to a lack of it, one has the memories of the past. Everything is equal here, you will not be compensated anywhere. One gets accustomed to everything by and by, and once the nut is cracked the kernel tastes better in the end. Reared in our circumstances, one has no idea of circumstances as they are here. Close figuring, trade-unionism, those official's and gentlemen's absurdities, fall as the fog and even though you have an unpoetic existence, there is a future ahead of you in which you may be free to do as you wish. You will be amply repaid for your efforts, and the future of the tenth generation will have the better and rosier foundation. Now be sure to come and take a pretty and rich wife, for wealthy girls are quite rare here. Pretty ones are as plentiful as there, but often they have no money—with 15% interest you could live well with a few thousand. Your women will not be able to ward off homesickness at first, but time brings roses and women are carried on one's hands, not because of a shortage of them but perhaps only because of well-meant gallantry which John Bull [i.e., the English] has brought across and with which he has inoculated the Irishman and the Dutchmen in time. This eases all things. The women have their own salons on the ship, are given preference everywhere, and everyone gladly gives them his place. I was once at a circus in Detroit that was so filled that no one was able to move. There came a young miss, and truly, a man who had paid his admission had to get out and let the lady in. That is how it is on the omnibus train, ships, in short, all over, as long as a woman looks well dressed. Well! This is the last side! Give my regards to Madame Knapp and Mr. Dierolf and greet Mr.

Hanx and wife, and say "How you do" to Worstly, and tell him that I live here among all the "damned beefsteaks." Also, Max Reichert, Ostermeyer and the little ones. If the world ever becomes too small for Max, he should write to me. America would be the place for him. . . .

J. Kerler, Jr.[32]

George Adam Fromader was another German immigrant who wanted to ease his countrymen's transition to the Wisconsin frontier. In 1846, the thirty-five year old moved from Bernstein, Bavaria, to Jefferson City (now Jefferson), Wisconsin, with his wife and three children. In this letter to his friend Johann Balthaser Koenig of Arzberg, Bavaria, George describes life in the Wisconsin German American community and compares his new surroundings with his homeland. Fromader had no regrets about choosing to live in Wisconsin and rhapsodized about the freedom he found in America. The letter was originally written in German.

Jefferson City
Jan. 15, 1847

. . . Here in America one eats meat every day, sometimes twice—mornings and evenings we have coffee. The Americans have meat on the table three times a day and many kinds of vegetables which we do not know of in Germany. The bread is made of the finest wheat flour, baked with leaven, and there is no trouble in getting yeast to bake fried cakes. On Saturday evening everybody makes fried cakes for Sunday. For coffee we usually exchange eggs, for 1 doz. eggs you get a pound of coffee. . . .

On Oct. 25, our son John and his betrothed Elizabeth Zeidler were married. Also John Adam Jahn was married, both of the weddings were at our house. So we had a joyful wedding celebration. On November 21 our young wife gave birth to a girl, to our great joy. They are both quite well and sound. We are all well and live very happily together. We do not care to be back in our unhappy Germany. There we would have had to waste many words and coax the law court and community officials to give permission for the marriage. In this country everybody is free to do as he pleases as long as he remains orderly and respectable. Hunting is permitted for everybody in places not fenced in, even on Sunday in the country. Hunting is forbidden in town during church hours.

In Germany we hear strange things about being hanged in America for stealing 5¢ worth of goods, but nobody here knows anything about that. Unless blood is shed, there is little conflict with the law. Everything is very closely investigated before any one is sentenced to prison. Few people let things go that far, for they cherish personal honor and like to have the confidence of their fellow men. An American is ashamed even to quarrel with others, let alone to resort to violence. If a person finds something, he avoids taking it home, but takes it to the nearest house to make it public. So there is the greatest order in everything.

In art and science the land is astonishingly far advanced, and in all things the Germans are far behind and acknowledge it readily. The country at large has already made great advancement in arts and science, over which the people rejoice generally. But the Germans have much to learn.

For church and school we can go to Jefferson. Every 2 weeks a clergyman comes to us and preaches in some private home, which, of course, seems very strange to us.

I can tell you, friends, whoever can bring into the country $200 in cash can become a prosperous farmer. He can buy 40 acres of land. If it is priced at 10 schillings, $100 is enough. For another $100 he can buy the most necessary equipment. And if he has grown-up children they can easily help their father, for here there is no scarcity of work and income, especially for women and girls. A girl of 9 or 10 years can earn a few dollars a month, at the same time she attends school. A good hired man or maid, here called help, each can earn monthly 8, 10, to 12 dollars, the sum depending on how he adapts himself to the work. Men and women have the same opportunity. In this country there is no distinction between master and servant at the table. Caste is unknown in this country. Nothing is known about nobility and different names and titles. Everybody enjoys the same respect, whether he be a servant, a farmer, a minister or a president. Honor is granted to all if deserved. Everybody works. People work for each other, all for pay. Nothing is known about the forester's work, which is considered the hardest in Germany. Every man here is a marksman and carries his gun. . . .

You dear friends, good night!
I have accomplished the voyage
That I intended to take
And have come to a good land.
I thank God for this way
Of getting a free life.
I have much wood and good land,
Were you here you would have it, too.
I live here happily
And wish you could have it the same way.
Good night, all you friends!
Germany is a vale of tears.[33]

European immigrants set about creating communities that blended elements of their European traditions with their American surroundings. The next two letters describe these new communities as they stood in the mid-nineteenth century. The first comes from the pen of the Reverend Wilhelm Streissguth (1827–1915) of the Swiss settlement of New Glarus and is addressed to the Magistrate Peter Jenny. As the president of the emigration society of Canton Glarus, Switzerland—the organization responsible for the settlement of New Glarus, Wisconsin—Magistrate Jenny circulated copies of letters from Swiss immigrants now living in Wisconsin for prospective colonists to see. The second letter is from Anders Jensen Stortroen to his family in Tönset, Norway. Stortroen describes the conditions at Martell Township in western Wisconsin from the home of Karl Olsen Bergebakken, a Norwegian settler. Both offer depictions of communities similar to those that blossomed all over Wisconsin during the nineteenth century. Streissguth's letter was originally written in German; Stortroen's was written in Norwegian.

To Herr Peter Jenny, Magistrate in Schwanden, President of the Hon. Emigration Society of Canton Glarus.

New Glarus,
Sept. 12, 1850

. . . The extent to which immigration to Wisconsin increases, borders on the incredible, still since one sees it daily he is bound to believe it. In Milwaukee alone, to say nothing of the other lake ports and of the immigration overland and up the Mississippi, in Milwaukee alone hundreds land daily and move out upon the so-called highways, in various directions, to the interior. Just now the principal movement seems to be more into the districts north of the river Wisconsin and to Lake Winnebago, probably because in our region nearly all good lands have been bought up by speculators, which can always be taken as a testimony in favor of the region.

But it is not alone European immigrants who move to Wisconsin, but very many farmers from the states who follow the wholly characteristic "Yankee-impulse" which drives them ever farther into favorable stretches of the West, so that the recent increase of population in the states of Wisconsin, Iowa, Missouri, and others is tremendous. I am convinced that Wisconsin, which is already like a wild garden, in ten years will become a blooming grain and fruit garden, and the early immigrants will then be richly rewarded for their labors. . . .

It is, therefore, easy to understand with what eager expectations I entered the colony and also, in view of such a background, with what a beating heart I hailed my future pastorate. That, upon the first meeting, I found no ground for affirming the views gathered at home has already been intimated. However, I thought, "All are now in their Sunday best," and the motto runs, "The new broom sweeps clean." Still, both the country and the people had already gained from me a certain measure of confidence. The first glimpse of the town did me good. The houses were of logs, to be sure, but I had already accustomed myself to the appearance of log houses. There were certainly no so-called "farm houses," as in other new villages. For these farm houses, from the beginning, have not pleased me, being drafty, flimsy, and shaky structures. If one imagines that living in a loghouse must be somewhat hard and uncomfortable, he will doubtless

Wilhelm Streissguth. WHI IMAGE ID 42740

find it so. Yet, if one enters into the conditions as they really are, one can live quite comfortably and happily in them.

I lived four weeks in Herr Tschudy's log house and, on account of the heat, I put up my bed for two weeks in the hay mow of the stable, where I slept splendidly on a hay mattress: and I found living in a log house by no means so bad, possessing a contented, easily gratified disposition. I must give the colonists high praise for having, up to now, possessed and maintained this contentedness. They have steadily kept in view the things that were most necessary, namely, preparing for cultivation a sufficient quantity of land, and with great satisfaction I observed on my visits to the individual, scattered homes, that every log house was surrounded with large stretches of beautiful, fertile land that gave plenty of evidence of the occupants' industry and endurance. Even well-to-do English[-speaking] farmers, if they are wise, begin with a log house, exchanging it for a better one only when the surrounding improved land justifies. Improvements, enlargements, are already beginning here and there, and in a few years most of the old dwellings will certainly disappear. Certain well-to-do farmers have already constructed stately buildings: for example, both Peter Jennies, of Wart and von Sool, Nik. Elmer, Jak. Ott, etc.

Similarly in regard to clothing, about which in the old home fable-makers bandy the words "tattered," "half-naked," and the like. On Sundays I find the people, without exception, properly, though to be sure very simply, attired. On working days one of course occasionally encounters vagrant fashion plates, and even garments through which sun and moon can shine cheerily. But, I know not whether because of my own content-edness or other people's discontentedness, I am not able to judge these conditions as severely as some have done. If one wants comparisons, he has but to observe all western farmers, poor and rich, also most towns-people, and he will see few different sorts of clothing on work days. No one is embarrassed to let the glorious sun shine on knees and elbows, as well as on hands and face.

To be sure, one sometimes sees the English ladies faring forth ostenta-tiously, but every honest German and Swiss is indignant at the peacock-like strutting of the American "ladies" who try to resemble a certain type of lower creature. If one bestows upon some of this showy apparel a closer examination, one will truthfully say that even a patched and mended New Glarus kirtle is better than such a threadbare, fluttering garment.

Every field and woods worker knows that the hard, rough labor to be performed here is not especially favorable to the wearing quality of cloth-ing. A suit that would last a whole year in a factory goes to pieces here in a few weeks in the struggle with severe storms, downpours of rain, dew and fog, thorns and brush, particularly if a vigorous, active and industrious body is inside it earnestly trying to support a numerous family and having from 20 to 30 acres of land to cultivate. In addition to all this, the purchase of clothing here is very costly, not so easy as in a manufacturing region like Glarus.

Oh! one does not need to pity our colonists so much on account of clothing. Rather should we pity those who, in the shade of a factory easily earn themselves money and as lightly spend it for clothing and other goods, live in fine two and three story houses—and when a sudden reverse in business ensues, have to exchange good living for poor, conceal a hungering body in fine raiment and find every difficulty in meeting the high house taxes. Our New Glarus people solace themselves with the thought of their gradual rise, one with another. They achieve for themselves a debt-free comfortable home, and look confidently to the future when they shall be able without anxiety to care for their bodies.

I hardly know whether to particularly contradict once more the accusation that some of the colonists are without means of subsistence. I of course do not know where such comments originate, but this I know, and am daily witness of, that they are perfectly absurd. I am convinced that most people at home experience more days of hunger in a single month than here in a whole year. No; of hunger days nothing at all is to be said. Flour, milk, potatoes, meat, butter, cheese, eggs, etc., are at hand in richest profusion. . . .

Wilhelm Streissguth, Pastor[34]

[Fall 1858]

[Martell Township, Wisconsin]

Dear Parents, Brothers and Sisters!

. . . Since we have been in America about ten months, and have traveled extensively both in Illinois, and now in different places in Wisconsin, we will this time give you as exact information as possible as to how America really is, and also concerning conditions here, as accurately as we have discovered them to be in every particular at these places. You must excuse us for not having fully informed you about this before, but we have not had any actual experience, and did not want to write what others have told us.

It is hard for one here in America to write a letter to you in Norway and take the responsibility for having written too much or too little, but put it down exactly as it is here, because if any of you should get the desire to follow us to America on account of these letters, and they did not describe conditions as they are here, we would consider ourselves unfortunate in that we have led anyone astray. But we will describe things in this letter as accurately as possible and as we understand them, then each and every one must do as they like, whether they wish to come to America or not.

We will first tell you about the country, and we can say at once that it is a very fertile land, as one can sow almost what kind of seed he chooses, and he will be certain that it comes up, and just as certain that it will not freeze down again. Neither is there any trouble with fertilizing for any type of farming, as it is unnecessary. Here the land is uniformly level except for small hills and valleys, so one place looks like another wherever one goes. In this locality the water is just as wholesome and good as in Norway, there being no difference. But as far as the woods are concerned, they are unpraiseworthy, since here no trees but oaks can be found, and they are not very plentiful on the farms the Norwegians have bought lately; but some of the Americans who settled here first have much woods and of the best quality, and they naturally did not settle in the poorest places. For they found both the most convenient locations and the best forests.

Their meadows consist of prairies and sloughs. Prairies are large level stretches where one cannot see forests in any direction while standing in the midst of the prairies, but can see only the blue rim of the sky around. And the sloughs are like the marshes in Norway as they are on wet land. And both kinds of meadows bear large crops, yes, fully as large as the luxuriant grass in Norway. Still, some of the Americans broke up land and seeded timothy seed which gives extremely high yields, and which is the best and most nourishing hay crop here also. What we call a "gaard" in Norway is called a farm here, and a large farm here consists of a dwelling house, a cellar and a stable. And here can be found many who have lived in America three or four years who do not yet have any house but live in cellars dug out of the ground. Fine houses are built mostly of timbers (logs), but they do not bevel the logs here as in Norway, but they let the logs lie as they first fall, then they take stones or whatever is most convenient and chink between the logs, later working together clay and lime and plastering the walls, and with that they are ready. And the roofs of the houses are of boards, since here neither birch bark, sod or stone (slate) are used for roofs. Some of the Americans have houses which are built of sawed lumber, which are large and fine. (There are enough buildings here after a fashion (if one could only thrive in such, which is the most difficult for all who come here).)

The winters here are neither as long or as cold as in Norway, and houses are needed for neither wheat or corn, as they make a box of boards in the field to put the crop in, cover it with straw for a roof, where it can stand until they haul it away and sell it. They haul their hay together and put it in stacks near their stables—those who have stables, otherwise a large number of the cattle spend the winter in the open.

The Norwegian farmers here have generally from 80 to 160 acres land, and an acre consists of about three Norse "maal." This is all their property, where they have their fields, their meadows and their pastures, likewise their woods, which will hardly suffice for many, to furnish enough building material, fuel and fences. From 10 to 40 acres of each farm have been cleared and put under cultivation, according to means. And the cultivated land is used to raise all kinds of crops.

On this much land one can live very peaceably and comfortably when he is not in debt. It is not much better to be [in] debt here than in Norway. For from 10 to 30 per cent interest is charged here, and summons and auctions occur here as well as in Norway. There are taxes and expenses for the farmer here as in Norway, although not as large. As far as earnings are concerned, there is a great deal of difference between here and Norway, since here a common laborer gets from 50c to $1.50 per day at this time,—it differs with the different kind of work and the hours are from six or seven a.m. to seven or eight p.m. the year around, as the days here are almost the same length all the time, and the nights are as dark the year around as they are in the fall over there.

There has been a serious financial depression here this year, as the wheat has been very cheap so wages have been generally lower than usual. There is better pay here for any kind of an artisan than for a common laborer; (although we have not worked at our trade for others very much, but have done only what was needed for ourselves, because) but one must learn to speak English well before one can carry on competently as a craftsman. . . .

We will tell you a little about religion which may cause you to reflect, when you hear how different it is in this part of the world in that respect. There are many different religions here, and one has the opportunity to embrace which ever one he chooses. One can hear a preacher here six times a year at most when one is in the vicinity, although we have not heard a minister preach more than two times since we were in Norway, as we have been absent on journeys. Religious services are held at the homes of the farmers in turn, as they do not have a church here, although we have seen several churches around here. But there is talk of building a church here also, in time, as they have fenced in a church yard this summer and have already dedicated it, so in time it will be a little more cheerful in that respect.

Here are also Norwegian schools (though not arranged like those in Norway) so those who want to educate their children and bring them up in a God-fearing manner have the opportunity to do so; but here are found many of those who are so indifferent that they attend neither religious services or school, as there is no compulsion in such cases. Still, one can lead as Christian a life here as in Norway if he chooses to do so (although it is really more difficult).

There are many, entirely too many temptations here, and many tempters who will lead one astray. On the other hand, there are few counselors here in America to comfort and guide one on the path which leads to Eternal Life and Salvation, as compared with where you are. And we will remind you, relatives and acquaintances at Faaset, that if any of you should desire to come to America, do not delude yourselves into the belief that you will hear as many good admonitions as you have heard, and will hear, at Faaset, for you will surely miss them.

As concerns the weather, there has been an excessive amount of rain and thunder this spring and summer, so no one can remember the like of it. Likewise, the heat was so intense the last part of June, that it was almost impossible to work at all. If we sat down in the shade, the sweat drops ran off our clothes like hail, and we had to change shirts two and three times each day. One can not work outside in the rain here, either, for it will bring on illness; so you must not estimate earnings for each day here.

For the sake of room we must close our humble letter although we have not written one tenth of what we would say had we been there. But a word more: that there is a great deal of difference, both in mode of living and profits, compared to Norway, you may be sure of, if one only can thrive here.

Anders Jensen Stortroen[35]

Settlers needed to focus on the basics—food, weather, and health—in order to survive the pioneer experience. Immigrants from abroad faced the added challenge of learning a new language, but all had to deal with feeling homesick and missing familiar faces and places. Some emerged energized and optimistic, others regretted their decision to migrate, and a few others even returned home. For those who remained and survived, there was the challenge and excitement of building something new, whether it was a farmstead, a marriage, or new customs and institutions.

3

"I PREFER AMERICA"

Building New Lives

After completing their trip to Wisconsin and making the initial adjustments to life in the West, pioneer settlers began to shape a way of living that was a hybrid of the old and the new. Settlers came from various parts of the United States and Europe, bringing with them their own assumptions, values, and cultures. Yet within this variety, there were some common themes. Cultural building blocks—family, religion, traditional folkways, and legal institutions—helped forge new communities in Wisconsin. As this excerpt from Christian Traugott Ficker's 1853 German-language handbook for prospective immigrants suggests, the first task for any settler was to find a way to earn a living. (For background on Ficker and his guide, see pages 8–9.) Ficker warned his fellow countrymen of the dangers of keeping old world assumptions in a new land.

Here the new immigrant must set himself the serious question: "What shall I do now?" If a craftsman, and you desire to pursue your craft in this country, look about and see if you can find a position in some workshop. Consider however, that though you may have been the most skillful worker in your trade in Germany, you will be able to create very little sensation therewith, but must learn above all that here for the most part everything goes faster and with improved tools. Do not therefore preen yourself upon your knowledge and skill but learn and be content at first with minimum wages. Do not imagine that when you step upon American soil the people will marvel at you, as such an extraordinary worker, such a knowing artist, or so great, a scholar; over you and your work, your artistic productions, or the fruits of your learning. There are plenty of extraordinary men of all classes in America. Hence, be not vain or puffed up, through which you can make yourself a laughing stock; rather—learn, and in time you will do right well.

It has often happened that immigrants came here and were unable to enter at once upon the trade they had learned and followed in Germany. In that case, friend, if you don't want to lie at the margin of subsistence, take any work which offers that you can do and which will furnish support. Do not fancy that people in America are so narrow in their sympathies as to judge a man by the coat he wears or the trade he follows, and on those accounts to appreciate or despise you. Here all are equal—all are citizens, from the president down to the wood chopper. I have seen people in Milwaukee in finest frock coats and black, silken vests, who were smoothing the earth with a shovel which was brought in by draymen to fill in the streets. That does not disgrace them here and no one regards it. One supports himself honestly thereby—that is sufficient!—Be it in the office with a pen—be it on the street with shovel in hand!—Be sensible; stop being a German and be an American.—True, this is not possible for everyone who has just come from Germany and cannot as yet forget the fact. He still lacks that independent, self-determined aptness in all relationships which from youth upwards so notably characterizes the resourceful American. Hence, it is not often the case that things suit the new immigrant at first blush. He comes here with too sanguine hopes, still too much in love with his old German, dearly-won institutions, thinks back on those only, and is deaf and blind to the new, the better; sees everything through foggy glasses and reasons falsely; the language, the climate, the mode of subsistence, the people, and a thousand other things are strange and unfamiliar to him. He becomes depressed, makes comparisons between the old and the new fatherland, overlooks the good and wholesome things of America and the doubtful disadvantageous things of Germany, and reasons in prejudiced, false fashion. This is the source of the numerous jeremiads intoned by new immigrants and sent back to Germany. It is the cause of the violent contradictions between the informant, for whom everything did not at once succeed, and who, with greatest exertions, could not immediately secure paying work, and therefore made America out to be unconscionable bad, and the one who was fortunate in finding at once upon arrival a good situation and therefore praised the country unreasonably.

Therefore, friend, learn to know America somewhat and get your affairs somewhat arranged before writing home to condemn the new fatherland or belittle its advantages. . . .

In purchasing a farm or vacant land, wherever possible you should take with you an experienced, understanding friend who has been in America for some time to assist you. He, too, may be overwhelmed by the scandalous, cunning deceptions, but you much more so. He will be more familiar with the speech than you, he can at least take you to the right place for finding out the truth about the condition of the land you are inclined to buy: whether it actually belongs to the person who wants to sell to you, whether or not a debt stands against it, and so on. In Germany, if one wishes to purchase a house or a piece of ground, he is informed by the magistracy what damages, debts, etc., are recorded against it. Here, however, that is unfortunately not the case: the authorities here go no farther than you demand and for which you pay them. For the rest, it is easy to see that purchases in well-settled districts are associated with less danger of swindling because there everyone knows, and it is easy to find out what conditions exist in connection with this or the other piece of land. On the other hand, in a poorly-settled region a settler sometimes does not know to whom the land adjoining his own belongs, since it lies vacant, without cultivation or occupancy; or whether it actually belongs to the person who does live upon it.

A great mistake of newly arrived immigrants is their strong mistrust of everyone who would serve them here with good advice. True, there are in America scoundrels in plenty who would like to skin the immigrant, who do not spare their neighbor or even their friend. But to trust and believe no one is to go too far and to throw out the baby with the bath. I have given my best advice to many a 'greenhorn' just as if he were my brother but I observed that he did not trust me. Mostly they have later regretted this often have told me they would have done better had they followed my advice. . . .

I said above that he who comes here and has money enough to buy an improved farm will find no great difficulty in carrying on his business. One need not think that the cultivation of land here is carried on in so sys-

131

HOMESTEADS

FOR SALE,

COMPRISING A LARGE NUMBER OF VERY DESIRABLE

VILLAGE LOTS,

Well located for Business purposes, or

PRIVATE RESIDENCES,

SITUATED IN THE

Village of Madison,

WISCONSIN.

Also, One Hundred and Fifty

FIVE and TEN ACRE LOTS, adjoining the Corporation
limits, within a few rods of the

Madison Mills and Water Power;

Possessing a FERTILE SOIL—fronting on HANDSOMELY
LAID-OUT AVENUES—well supplied with

WOOD, WATER, &c.

Surrounded by beautiful LAKE SCENERY, and affording
a fine View of the

VILLAGE AND STATE CAPITOL.

TERMS AND CONDITIONS OF SALE.

Actual residence and immediate improvement, credit from one
to ten years, to suit purchasers, and a PERFECT TITLE given.
For particulars enquire of

L. J. FARWELL,

Office, Bank Building, Pinkney st., Madison, Wis.

Land advertisement of Leonard Farwell appearing in an 1855 Madison city directory. WHI IMAGE ID 38583 tematic a manner, or that everything concerning it is so carefully studied, as in Germany. This cannot be, as everyone will see after I have set forth for his benefit, as briefly as possible, the plan and method of cultivation.

As soon as the immigrant has bought himself a tract of forest land (covered with tall, slender oak, sugar maple, hickory, walnut, and linden trees that indicate good soil) and has built upon it the necessary dwelling for himself and family, he begins to cut down trees, after he has gathered together what already lies on the ground and has thrown it in heaps. In order to bring a certain regularity into the business, it is necessary that he should not cut down a new tree until he has trimmed the preceding one and cut it into sections or logs, 12-14 feet long (depending upon the thickness of the stem), so that a single pair of oxen can drag them away. The stumps are left standing until, after a few years, they rot and crumble of themselves, or at least are easily removed. It is easy to see that such a field does not make a very good impression on a new immigrant. As I was coming by train from Albany to Buffalo and saw the many stumps in many fields, I thought: "Must not these be lazy people? In my field these stumps shall not remain. I shall remove them 'root and branch.'" That is what they all think who see these for the first time, yet later they all let the stumps stand in their fields until they are pretty well rotted. And that is the right way.

He who begins in June, July, August, September, and so on (in which months most of the immigrants arrive) to cultivate a farm, must set about to clear some land on which to sow winter grain in order that the following year he may have a harvest and will not be required to buy his bread and other necessities a second year. Now how long would it require to take the stumps out of an acre of land! Within this time he could at least clear ten acres which would provide him more grain, and in this manner his farm would come to something near completedness, in a much shorter time. To have the trees with the stumps grubbed out by hired help would be very costly, for wages here are high, and it is not possible to hire a hand in summer under four or five shillings together with free board and washing, or by the year under $80-$100. On the prairies where farmers often own several hundred, yes even thousands, of acres, hired men never receive less than $120 and often $150 and more per year. When the farmer has acquired some buildings and is not inclined to cut down more of his woodland, he then considers the question of getting out his stumps, whereby, of course, the value of his land is enhanced. In this neighborhood, at the present time, where farmers have lived for sometime, their fields are quite clear of stumps.

As soon as a certain area of woods is cut down and made into short lengths, the brush that has been piled up is first burned off. Then the farmer obtains the assistance of several strong men and one or two yoke of strong oxen, if he does not have them himself. The oxen drag the logs together, and the men roll them in piles after which they are burned. Of course, somebody must always be in attendance to pull the burning sticks together in order that they may be entirely consumed. Often as many as twenty or thirty acres are in flames at the same time which gives to the night a peculiarly brilliant appearance and seen from afar is not unlike a military camp. This being accomplished, all scattered light stuff is brought together and burned, the land fenced, seeded, and harrowed several times.[36]

As Ficker points out, immigrants had to decide how to earn a living and, if farmers, how to adapt to American agricultural practices. The following two letters, one from Johann Frederick Diederichs and the other from John Kerler Sr., describe their efforts to begin farms in Wisconsin.

Diederichs, who had emigrated from Germany to Manitowoc in 1847, was awestruck by the natural environment in America, where everything seemed larger. He admitted that his first year in America was his hardest, but he did not regret emigrating. (For background on Diederichs, see page 44.)

John Kerler Sr. (1800–1885), a successful brewer and former magistrate from Memmingen, in Bavaria, moved to Wisconsin in 1849 and settled in Greenfield west of Milwaukee with his sons and daughters and his hired man, Elias. His son John Kerler Jr. had gone ahead of the family and purchased land. (See pages 87–89 for the letter of John Kerler Jr.) The European revolutions of 1848 rocked the German states, leading to the emigration of many failed rebels to America. Describing life on his farm, John Kerler Sr. still yearned to live in "civilized, cultured Germany" in its "former orderly condition," but he, too, was ready to throw his lot in with America. Together, the two letters offer a view of some immigrants' struggles to establish working farms in Wisconsin. Both letters were originally written in German.

[Manitowoc] Rapids
May 21, 1848.

. . . We had a mild winter this year, and only a few days when the snow could withstand the sun; it rained but little and I do not believe that on the whole we had fourteen days when it was not possible to work. As a general rule all natural phenomena in America are on a grand scale. When it does storm, you hear a crashing in the forest as if there were cannon booming; trees are uprooted and fall with thunderous din upon others, taking their branches with them. During such a storm no one ventures into the woods. Altogether, there is a strangeness about the "Bush." Of paths there is no thought and it is therefore easy to get lost, and one is not able to find his way again unless he takes as his guide the sun by day and the moon by night, if they be visible. Therefore every one must consider it his duty, before retiring, to step outside and listen, to hear whether any one is calling; that this practice is of benefit was recently proved to us by August Poetz, who was coming from the Rapids, had been delayed and lost his way, and would have been forced to camp in the woods over night if his call had not reached me. We are the outermost settlers here, and how far to the south and west of us there are people living we do not know. A. Poetz and Grauman, of Iserlohn, are now here to build a log house on their forty-acre tract located about ten minutes from us; Poetz, however, with wife and children will remain in Milwaukee, intending to come here after the opening of navigation. The family has thus far not prospered, since work is scarce in Milwaukee this winter; I believe, however, it will be better next summer in Manitowoc or the Rapids, where there is much building.

As yet Wisconsin has very few churches and schools, for the state is just beginning to flourish; but Milwaukee, after eleven years' existence, already has 15,000 inhabitants, some twenty churches—seven of them Lutheran, and nearly all differing among themselves. It seems as though our state will in time become predominantly German, for my countrymen already constitute a majority of the population and in Milwaukee there is more German than English spoken. . . .

My dear wife has planted the garden; I have seeded a tract with corn and beans, and, God willing, shall plant potatoes and sow corn and oats this week—I am writing this on May 15th. With Fred and Carl I am now busy building a fence around the cleared land, which will be finished to-morrow and whose purpose is to keep swine and other animals off the land. My two boys afford me genuine joy, and I assure you that if I did not have them I should never get through, for it is in fact no trifling matter, and many a person, if he knew what it means to be a farmer, would con-sider it ten times before he left Europe. However, I do not for a moment regret that I am here, because I am convinced (humanly speaking) that my future will brighten, although my children will have the real benefit of it.

The first year is, of course, the hardest, when everything must be pur-chased; yet, as an example, I am now raising all our provisions and hope to have some for sale next year; every year more land will be cleared and consequently more harvested. To tell the truth, I must say that whoever has money and the inclination to be a farmer can do no better than to come here; and when I think of some of my friends who are daily putting their little money into risky speculations, I am moved to exclaim: "Oh, if you but knew that, with the smallest capital, you could gain a competence here that would assure the safest, simplest, and most quiet life!"

He who settles on wild land should have about $500; but for $2000 one can at any time buy the finest farms, with all livestock and with provisions for one year (for people and cattle), and I should like to know what more can be desired. Likewise in money matters—the lowest interest is twelve per cent, with the best security; also much money is to be earned in trade, and if I had the means I should import some ribbons, sewing implements, and buttons, and feel sure of great profits. Otherwise it is necessary to have for trade a knowledge of the English language and of the best sources of supply. Finally, I want to report that since yesterday our woods are full of pigeons, coming in great swarms, covering this entire region; they are very palatable and we could shoot them at our pleasure if we only had the time for it. There is a tradition current here that the region where the pigeons appear will that same year be fully occupied by human beings, which, if that should really occur here, would be great luck for us; for then, natu-rally, our property would rise greatly in value. And now, to the faithful God, before whom we shall all be united again, may you all be committed.

Joh. Fr. Diederichs[37]

Milwaukee
November [1849]

Dear cousin!

... My farm is 2 ½ hours west of Milwaukee, has a very nice location and lies between two roads, one of them covered with planks. The entire surroundings consist of rolling hill country which, for the most part is covered with the best soil. My property consists of 200 acres, 50 acres of which are meadow with superior grass, mostly red clover, 40 acres of [uncultivated] fields, 10 acres of potatoes, maize and turnips, and 100 acres of woods with mostly sugar maples, mixed with oaks, linden and nut trees. The maples promise a rich sugar harvest for the next year. A small creek flows from north to south through my property in front of the house. Our neighbors are mostly Germans, just as in Milwaukee, and this is not without value to us. My buildings consist of a log house and a couple of huts. The first had to be built a little bigger so that all of us would have living room. In addition, we built a stall for two horses, a barn with cattle stalls underneath, 50 feet long and 30 feet wide and large enough for 22 head of cattle, and a two-story dwelling, 22 feet long by 23 feet wide, with a cellar. There was much work. Wood boards and shingles were carried to the building site with two horses and four oxen. Field stones, some so large that two persons had to lift them, were collected on the property and used as walls in the barn and cellar, and now perhaps for the first time in their lives the cattle are in a barn. The Americans leave their cattle out in the open, summer and winter, so that the milk often is frozen in the udder. I could not bring myself to do that, so that the cattle barn was first to be erected. A garden will be planted in the spring with manure-bed for early crops, which find an excellent market and are well paid for in Milwaukee. Last year's harvest consisted of wheat, oats, potatoes, maize, turnips, hay and straw. We also had 10 head of cattle, 18 pigs, 20 hens, 2 guinea hens, 13 turkeys, 8 geese and 11 sheep. I paid $17 per acre. My household works efficiently and are healthy and cheerful. The girls and one maid take care of the house, kitchen and poultry, and Edward, Louis and Elias do the other work. John takes care of the purchases in the city, and Herman's favorite occupation is to drive four oxen that follow him on the English command in woods and fields without a halter. He calls "ha, tschi, oha" all day and often in his sleep.

Just as in Germany I meet satisfied and dissatisfied people here, many who like it and many who long to be back in Germany. . . .

I would prefer the civilized, cultured Germany to America if it were still in its former orderly condition, but as it has turned out recently, and with the threatening prospects for the future of religion and politics, I prefer America. Here I can live a more quiet and undisturbed life. One lives in such safety here in the country that you seldom lock your door at night, leaving cattle, wagons, plows, everything out in the open without having to fear thievery. At most, delicacies such as smoked meat, fruit and the like, are stolen.[38]

Most letters written by men stressed the details of starting a farm, the prices of land and commodities, and the prospects for economic success. Letters from women such as Veronica Kerler Frank (1828–1864) often focused on domestic matters. The daughter of John Kerler Sr. (whose letter appears immediately above), Veronica was twenty-four at the time of her letter-writing in 1852 and had recently married August Frank. August owned a dry goods store in Milwaukee and had also emigrated from Germany. Writing to her new in-laws in Germany, Veronica describes her wedding, her household, and the everyday life of a German immigrant woman in Wisconsin. The exuberant new bride is enamored with her husband's beard and says she hopes he keeps it so she can "zobel" him. While the word literally means "sable," she likely means playfully teasing him by pulling his beard. The letter was originally written in German.

Milwaukee

August [1852]

. . . Yes, I am very, very happy, and may my August always be made so by me. It is very quiet and tranquil in our little household, but also quite merry. August visits me as often as his business allows, since our living quarters are only one story above the store. I am always busy, since I am making my dowry, for August was in such a hurry to get married that I could hardly finish the most necessary things. Our engagement lasted only three weeks. We were married on July 18. This important day was spent quite gaily and pleasurably. In the morning at 8 o'clock, we drove to the church, one mile from our farm, where H. Koester, pastor of the Greenfield congregation, performed the ceremony and then had a sermon on the text chosen by us, Psalm 121, v. 1–8. (It was not necessary to be married by justice of the peace, also.)

After the service, we drove back to the farm. My sister and sister-in-law had returned right after the wedding and had prepared the meal in the meantime. After the dinner, we went for walks on the farm, then a table with wine and sweets was set out in the open, where it tasted doubly good. In the evening several songs were played on the organ, also out in the open, and so the day flowed along with joyful talk.

Besides my family, Pastor Koester and Mr. and Mrs. Goll were at the wedding. My brother drove us to our new house the next morning. I received a beautiful black silk dress as a wedding present from my dear August, which I wore on the wedding day along with a white blond long shawl and a myrtle wreath in my hair. August wore his good black pants and coat which he had brought from Germany, but had taken in to about half its size. My bridegroom pleased me very much with his nice blond beard. He must keep it as long as I am around him, for 1, he had it when we became acquainted, and 2, I would not be able to "zobel" him without it if he ever gets angry. Until now he was good and did not need to suffer these pains much. But back to the farm and to my family. You, dear father, desire an accurate description of it from August, but he asked me to do it, so: 1. my father, 52 years old, still well and jolly. He feels quite happy on his farm and is in his Elysium [i.e., Paradise] there as he has always been a great friend of agriculture. He always works in the fields, along with the other men, which gives him great pleasure. 2. My brother John, in Holland, [Michigan,] whom you have known for years. 3. Edward, 25 years old, who married a friend of mine from Memmingen last year. Her parents live in Sheboygan. 4. Louis, 22 years old, single, is still working for father, but will take over some of father's land since he has cleared 80 acres which he could never keep for himself. 5. My step-sister Regina, 24, who keeps house for my father now. 6. Herman, 12 years old, has been on the farm up until now but is supposed to come to us in the city this winter to go to school. It will be pretty gay in our house when dear Bertha and Herman get together, since both are quite talkative. 7. I, born February 28, 1828. Now, dear father, I ask you to be satisfied with this description for the present. I did it as well as I could. Now dear mother, it may interest you a little to know how our new household is arranged, so listen: In the morning at 6:30, I finally succeed in getting my sleepy-head (August) out of bed. He must first finish dressing, and build a fire in the stove until I come. At seven we drink coffee with butterbread and molasses, then August goes into his store and I into my rooms, which are two stairs above the kitchen. I have four of them. 1. The parlor, facing the marketplace, 2. then the bedroom, 3. a large dining room, 4. then a small guest room. There is a nice chest of drawers in the parlor, and a black-upholstered sofa, a stove, a rocking chair and four ordinary chairs, a small work-table and a large mirror. In the large room there is a high wardrobe, a table and two chairs. There is also a pulley, by means of which I can pull the food up from the kitchen to upstairs. At ten I go back into the kitchen to prepare the noonday meal. We usually have soup, meat and vegetable or roast, salad and coffee, or cutlets, birds, etc. After eating, I go into the parlor and sew until five, at which time August chases me back into the kitchen. For supper we have tea, butter, bread, molasses, pancakes or souffles, or other things. No matter what I bring to the table, I seldom take anything away, because of our good appetite. I had to take in August's vests six weeks ago, and now I am afraid I might have to let them out again soon. But no, I am not afraid, on the contrary, as long as he feels healthy with me in body as well as heart. We have visitors from the farm every week, since father must always come in for business reasons. I drive out with him every third week on Saturday, and on Sunday my dear August usually comes, too, and in the evening Hermann takes us half-way or all the way back into the city. On the other Sundays, which we spend in the city, we go to church in the morning to a Pastor Muehlhaeuser (a Wuerttemberger, who came about 16 years ago). In the afternoons August goes for a glass of beer and I keep myself occupied by reading, my favorite pastime on Sundays, and in the evening we sometimes take a nice walk along the lake. "Now it is all, what I know."

Now, my dear parents, accept my thanks once again for your great love and take my love as proof.

Your
devoted daughter[39]

Once the immediate demands of clearing the land, building shelter, and establishing a household were met, residents of early Wisconsin built community ties that reached beyond the close network of family and friends. Ethnic communities that spread across the state became an important element of Wisconsin's social fabric. Ole Munch Ræder, a Norwegian scholar who studied the settlements established by his countrymen in Wisconsin, sent his analysis home in the form of letters, which were published in the prominent Christiania (now Oslo) newspaper *Den Norske Rigstidende*. (For background on Ræder, see page 83.) Ræder describes the Norwegian American community in Wisconsin as it stood in 1847 and ponders its meaning to both the Norwegian settlements themselves and American society as a whole. In doing so, he wrestles with the strain felt by immigrants who wished to retain their ethnic identity while simultaneously assimilating into a new society. The letter was originally written in Norwegian.

The next day, which was Sunday, a driver called for us in the morning with a coach drawn by two horses and, after a drive of a couple of hours towards the southwest, we arrived at the Norwegian settlement at Muskego Lake. The first people whom we met were a couple from Tinn, both of whom seemed greatly pleased with the visit. True-hearted and simple, just as we find our countrymen here and there up among the mountains in Norway, they had preserved their customs, dress, and general arrangement of the house unchanged, as well as their language. They served us with excellent milk and whatever else they had; and, when they had become confident that we were altogether Norwegian, they also brought some excellent *flatbrød*, made of wheat, which they had at first held back because "these Yankees" are so ready to make fun of it. The Yankee who was with us, however, seemed very well pleased with it when we let him try it. On a later occasion we induced him to try another dish, just as Norwegian and just as unfamiliar to him, namely, *fløtegrøt*, which he declared "first-rate" as he licked his lips. Our friends from Tinn were well satisfied with their condition; they had managed so well during the first four years that they had paid off the debt that they had incurred and now they already had a little surplus.

We next visited, among others, Even Heg, who seems to be one of the leaders among the Norwegians in these parts. He is said to be a Haugean and he was away attending a devotional meeting when we reached his house. He, too, seemed satisfied with the state of his affairs. He did not feel very friendly towards Reiersen, who, in his opinion, had given exaggerated accounts of the unhealthful conditions at Muskego and had thereby frightened the later Norwegian immigrants to such an extent that they not only would not settle there but they even went miles out of their way to avoid going through the place. Mr. Heg, by the way, has earned the gratitude of the Norwegians in Wisconsin by starting a printing establishment on his own farm, with the assistance of Mr. Bache, a financier from Drammen, who lives with him. Here they publish the Norwegian-Wisconsin newspaper, *Nordlyset*, edited by Mr. Reymert. It is without doubt a very good idea through such a medium to maintain a cultural link between the Norwegians here and the mother country, as well as among themselves. Every one, indeed, who would like to see them preserve their national characteristics and their memories of their native land as long as possible must, first and foremost, turn his attention to the problem of preserving their language by keeping it constantly before their eyes and ears.

As you know, I cannot convince myself that all these countrymen of ours, as they leave our own country, are to be regarded as completely lost and as strangers to us. On the contrary, I believe that they are carrying on a great national mission—in accordance with the wishes of Providence, working through their instinctive desire to wander. Their mission consists in proclaiming to the world that the people of the Scandinavian countries, who in former days steered their course over every sea and even found their way to the distant shores of Vinland and Hvidmannaland, have not been blotted out from among the peoples of the earth, nor have they degenerated. After having regained their independence, so that they can show themselves in the world, they come to demand their place in that country upon which their fathers cast the first ray of light, no matter how flickering and uncertain, and to take part in the great future which is in store for this youthful, but already mighty, republic. Let them become Americans, as is the duty of holders of American soil, but this need not prevent them from remaining Norwegian for a long time to come. The American character is not yet so fixed and established that it excludes all others. The Americans are satisfied with demanding a few general traits of political rather than of really national significance. Under such lenient influences, the aliens are elevated and improved, rather than changed; they lose their sharp edges and adopt some of the good qualities of others. Even if America, fulfilling also in this respect a great and providential purpose, shall in the end absorb and mold together into a compact whole all the various nationalities which now are making their contributions in such rich measure, and shall not only blot out the many prejudices which now separate people in their home countries but also absorb some of the individual characteristics which now constitute the peculiar qualities of each nation, even if such be the case, then surely it will be for us, as well as for every other European nation, not merely a source of satisfaction as an historical fact, but perhaps also, in the course of events, a factor of real benefit that our Scandinavian North has become one of the parent nations for this nation to whose lot will undoubtedly some day fall the place of leadership in the affairs of the world. . . .

The ease with which the Norwegians learn the English language has attracted the attention of the Americans, all the more because of the fact that they are altogether too ready to consider them entirely raw when they come here. "Never," one of them told me a few days ago, "have I known people to become civilized so rapidly as your countrymen; they come here in motley crowds, dressed up with all kinds of dingle-dangle just like the Indians. But just look at them a year later: they speak English perfectly, and, as far as dress, manners, and ability are concerned, they are quite above reproach." Of course I tried to explain to him that their original mode of dress certainly could not make Indians out of them and that they were not entirely devoid of culture or those habits of diligence and reg- ularity which one expects to find in a well-ordered and civilized society, even among the poorest classes out in the country, but he seemed scarcely disposed to make any concessions on that point.

On the other hand, he did not seem to know a great deal about the Norwegians in this country. My impression, after many visits extending over a number of settlements, is that the great mass of the families have essentially changed very little. I shall not deny, however, that they have been able to meet the severe strain of the work with an iron will, and thus have had ample opportunity to strengthen their moral courage, and it also seems to be a fact that there is less drinking here than in Norway, although there are enough drunkards here, too, and among them some who have acquired the habit since they came here. Cleanliness is, here as in Norway, for many of them almost an unheard-of thing. The entrance to one of the houses I visited was guarded by a formidable cesspool. If a place looks really filthy and disreputable, you must expect to meet either Norwegians or Swiss or Irish ("Eirisa," as the Norwegians call them).

Of course there are some notable exceptions, but, on the whole, one must admit that it is particularly among young people who have gone into the service of Americans that one finds a real desire for improvement. This it is which makes the Norwegian name respected and almost loved here. This it is which has given our people such a general reputation for respectability, morality, sobriety, and natural ability that I frequently hear expressions to the effect that the whole of Norway might well come here and be received with open arms. On account of these qualities Norwegian young people are much in demand as servants. I believe there is not a single house of any size at all in Madison where Norwegians are not found. . . .

It is, on the whole, quite remarkable how quickly our farm-girls improve when they are out among strangers. Their English is quite correct, but as soon as they start to speak their mother tongue, it generally sounds broad and clumsy enough; no matter how much patriotic love you may profess to feel for the various dialects of our language, you cannot deny or at any rate avoid the feeling that the harmony is broken, even if the unfortunate expression comes from the fairest mouth or is animated by the friendliest smile. I believe that most of them are not conscious of the peculiar impression made by their way of speaking Norwegian; at any rate, they are too good-hearted and too happy in the recollection of their native land to be bothered by such a trifle. One can scarcely say as much for the Norwegian boys; at any rate, I have heard the opinion expressed that as soon as they have learned "to guess" and "to calculate," they at once become strangers to their less fortunate countrymen and are very loath to admit their Norwegian origin. This fact (and I am inclined to believe it is one) furnishes new proof of the need of improving the cultural conditions among our countrymen here and, at the same time, of increasing their national pride so much, at least, that they will not feel themselves tempted to deny their own country. I do not believe that any cultured Norwegian has ever felt any tendency to do such a thing; on the contrary he is all too apt to boast of the fact that he comes from the "land of the heroes." He realizes, at any rate, that his country, in spite of its poverty, has every claim to the respect of strangers; and he will not so easily be overwhelmed by the feeling of reverence for "these mighty Yankees," which seems to affect our simple countrymen so deeply and probably accounts for the fact that they make such good servants, much better, in fact, than they were in their own country. If this reverence could only reduce itself to a feeling of respect for the enterprise and other good qualities of the Yankees, then their desire to progress, instead of being mere servile imitation, would assume a somewhat more honorable aspect. Thus, instead of trying to lose themselves among the mass of strangers, as Jews do when they are converted, they would continue their relations with their countrymen, on whom they could thus exert a most beneficial influence.

They have all the more reason for assuming such an attitude because of the fact, as already indicated, that the Americans themselves certainly do not consider it a disgrace to be Norwegian. It cannot, of course, be said that they have any particular respect for the culture of the Norwegians or for their spirit of independence, a thing which is here considered of great importance as a civic virtue, because the sort of intelligence which is shown in a more or less successful attempt at imitation is always of a somewhat lower type. But as soon as the young people have risen from their present status as servants and have become independent farmers or shop-owners, and that time is not so far distant, then the Norwegians will without doubt enjoy the respect and confidence of their fellow-citizens, which will show itself through election to public offices—provided that they do not forfeit this good will by their own actions. . . .

As soon as a few such men have risen from their humble beginnings, the Norwegian name will undoubtedly win all the glory that can be desired. Already, as the account just given of the constitution affair shows, the Americans have begun to take official notice of the Norwegians. This is also seen in the names "Christiania" and "Norway" given to a couple of new towns.[40]

Like the immigrants from Europe, American-born settlers sought to transplant cultural values to Wisconsin. Moral and religious issues, especially those related to issues such as alcohol and slavery, caused

conflict among the settlers. Ministers of the Gospel saw Wisconsin as
a fertile ground for reform. The Reverend David Lowry (1796–1877),
a Presbyterian missionary from Kentucky, moved to Prairie du Chien
with his wife, Mary Ann, in 1833 to superintend an Indian school. In
this letter to *The Revivalist*, a Presbyterian newspaper published in
Nashville, Tennessee, Lowry describes what he feels are the moral
shortcomings of the Wisconsin frontier. Just as Catholic priests
brought negative attitudes about Protestants, Lowry had a similar low
opinion about Catholics.

Prairie Du Chien, Mich. Ter.
Nov. 22. 1833.

Dear Brother,—

Since my arrival at this place, I have tried to preach nearly every Sabbath, and am sure I never saw a place where the gospel was more needed.
Hunting and horse racing are quite common here, on the Lord's day, and
other kindred views equally prevalent. Several times I have witnessed from
my door on the Sabbath, a company of rational beings, assembled in the
Prairie, to enjoy what *they called*, the pleasure of seeing one little poney
run before another. I will remark, however, that most of these Sabbath
breakers are beyond the reach of my ministry; for they are Frenchmen,
and cannot understand a word of English, yet, their example will prove
ruinous to our American youth, of this place, unless it is counteracted
with the gospel. It would appear strange, were I to tell you that these very
characters are professors of the Holy religion of Jesus; but it is even so,
they are Roman Catholics.

My congregations have generally been small, but quite attentive and
serious. On last Sabbath, at the close of my sermon, a lady arose of her
own accord, at a distant part of the house, and came forward as a seeker
of religion, and gave me her hand; other sinners wept, and the people of
God were encouraged to hope for a revival.

There are several settlements, forty, and fifty miles distant, that are
very desirous for preaching, some of which I have visited. Schools too, are
greatly needed, and would be well supported could suitable teachers be
obtained. I have recommended an itinerant plan of school keeping, untill
a teacher can be provided for every neighborhood, that is, for one teacher

The Reverend David Lowry. WHI IMAGE ID 137174

to take charge of several neighborhoods, and travel from one to another spending a portion of time in each.

Should there be any young men of piety and enterprise within the limits of your acquaintance, who are out of business and wish to teach school, send them here, we will find them employment, and pay them well for it, for I know of no *new country*, where money is more plenty than it is here.

D. Lowry[41]

The temperance movement was one of the most hotly contested issues in early Wisconsin. The use of hard liquor was very popular during this period, and the average annual consumption of alcohol among adults was 7.1 gallons per American during the 1830s. The hard-drinking reputation of frontier areas such as Wisconsin presented temperance advocates like Lowry with an even greater challenge. His next letter to *The Revivalist* in Nashville describes the atmosphere of heavy drinking that often permeated the fringes of white settlements in Wisconsin.

Prairie Du Chien, Mich. Ter.

Dec. 7, 183[3]

Dear Brother,—The cause of temperance on yesterday, at this place, achieved a very triumphant victory. I delivered an address to a very large audience, composed, mostly of officers and soldiers of the garrison; at the close of which, I read a constitution, and received sixty pledges to abstain from the use of ardent spirits. Several officers joined, and were solicitous that their men should follow their example.

There is no place in the United States where the influence of the temperance enterprise is more imperiously called for than here. More ardent spirits are consumed, and there are more drunkards in this village than in any place I ever saw of the same population. Notwithstanding the special regulation of the war department, prohibiting the soldiers from drawing whiskey as a part of their rations, there are sometimes thirty and forty in the guard house at one time for getting drunk; and for several weeks passed, a guard has been regularly ordered, to prevent intercourse between the soldiers and the low dram shops of this place. How humiliating to see a man pacing all day before the door of a grog shop, with a musket on his shoulder, to prevent rational beings from poisoning themselves; and yet, after all of this precaution, drunkards and drunkenness are everyday multiplying.

Moreover, on the success of the temperance cause here, and another portions of our frontiers, hangs the last hope of the Indians. As long as white people continue to sell, they will purchase ardent spirits; and I am warranted in saying that, at the present time, most of their annuity is spent in this way, and they will continue this course so long as temptation is held up before them; or, until public sentiment closes the little whisky hovels, kept at our frontier villages.

D. Lowry.

P.S. As the above was not in time for the mail, it has been detained a week, during which, fifty five additional pledges have been given, making in all one hundred and fifteen. More than one half of the army here have now resolved to abstain from use of ardent spirits!!!

D.L.[42]

The Reverend Jeremiah Porter (1804–1893) was a Presbyterian minister, originally from Hadley, Massachusetts, who became a missionary evangelist of the American Home Missionary Society, an interdenominational organization that aided the establishment of Christian congregations on the frontier. Porter moved from Illinois to Green Bay in 1840 where he remained as a pastor until 1858. Jeremiah Porter was another Yankee reformer involved in the growing temperance movement, which opposed the drinking of alcohol. In this letter to the Reverend Milton Badger, the American Home Missionary Society's associate secretary, Porter relates his success in creating a temperance society in Green Bay. He refers to the Washingtonian movement, which promoted total abstinence from alcohol.

Green Bay W.T.
June 18 1842

Dear Mr. Badger

. . . Tho. I know not that I can report any conversions from sin to holiness, since the date of my last, which you have just published, immediately in town; Yet in distant settlements, in the bounds of this church, the Lord has been gathering some into his fold by the power of his own Spirit & in such a way as to glorify his own name; & in town, we have had a surprising & delightful Washingtonian triumph.

The overflowing eye, the half uttered groan of a full soul & the delightful spirit of christian fellowship, witnessed in our sanctuary & in our prayer meetings, has testified that God's refreshing, vivifying Spirit was still with us. And He hath heard us in producing a pleasing civil reformation which we trust confidently is making the paths straight for a still more delightful & radical moral reform. Our past revivals have prepared the way for the change which now rejoices this whole community, except those who deeply feel that the craft by which they have their wealth is in danger; & this change, we must believe, will be followed by a more extensive revival of pure religion than we have ever yet enjoyed. For this we are now praying & laboring, & as we thank God for the past we take courage for the future. We had for months desired a visit from some reformed inebriate, thinking then an impulse would begin to the cause of total abstinence, which we could not otherwise effect. But our isolated situation prevented the gratification of that wish. Although, however, the delightful reports that pound in upon us from abroad, in connection with the prayers of the people of God here, set the ball tardily in motion. At our first meetings, this spring, few were present but the old, tried friends of temperance, & some of the converts of last winter. But in a few weeks a band of men, of good minds & esteemed in the community (except for their unfortunate thirst for poison)—men whose lovely families had almost dispaired of earthly bliss, marched manfully up to the secretary's table, & pledged themselves solemnly before a delighted audience. That was a joyful night to our church & community. The influence of that scene spread like electricity around us. Hope to which many wives had been almost strangers, was lighted up in their hearts. Week after week the work went on, until almost every man that had been intemperate, & who has any self-respect has joined the happy ranks of the reformed. Our immediate influence has been more directly over the protestant population, tho. Many Catholics have joined our Society. Now, the Catholic Priest aided by the Bishop, at present here, is presenting the cause before his subjects, & tomorrow the Sabbath, he expects them in a mass to take the pledge. I am confident that a majority will do it, & it will be a triumphant day for this frontier, where Alcohol's seat has so long been. The poor Indians around us, many of them yet remain his victims. But temperance shall triumph & they shall be free.

An incident connected with our court which was recently in session will show something of the change in public opinion here. The grand jury

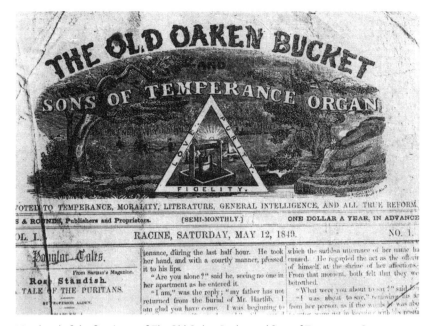

Masthead of the first issue of *The Old Oaken Bucket and Sons of Temperance Organ,* a Racine temperance newspaper, May 12, 1849. WHI IMAGE ID 67985

imposed a fine upon its members for late attendants of members. By this means a little sum had accumulated at the close of its sessions. The question then arose. What shall we do with it? Instead of expending it for wine & cigars one member moved it should be given to the Amer[ican] Bib[le] Society. The motion was seconded & passed unanimously! . . .

Ever Your Bro. in the Lord
Jeremiah Porter[43]

While temperance advocates such as Lowry and Porter achieved a moderate degree of success in eroding the hard-drinking reputation of the West, not everyone agreed with their policy on alcohol. The passage of a law in Maine in 1851 that banned the manufacture and sale of alcohol generated petitions to the legislature calling for Wisconsin's own version of a "Maine Law," largely from American-born Protestant citizens who had emigrated from New England and New York. The immigrant minority, especially those from Germany, led the opposition. The following two 1852 petitions made the case against prohibition. The first, from Washington County, was printed in both German and English, and provides an articulate and heartfelt opposition to prohibition in early Wisconsin. The text is taken from the English-language version of the petition. The second petition, from Lake Muskego in Waukesha County, used humor and ridicule to express the signers' views on prohibition. With tongue in cheek, the twenty signers of the imaginary "Muskego Lake Fishing Club" argued that a prohibition law would "multiply the water drinking classes of creation to such an awful extent," leading to a tragic series of catastrophes. Instead, they asked the legislature to pass a law banning the watering down of "*Good Liquor*." The legislature had received 3,829 signatures on petitions calling for prohibition and 3,742 signatures opposing it. Recognizing the divided opinion, the legislature called for an advisory referendum on prohibition to be put on the ballot in 1853, which passed 27,519 to 24,109. Nonetheless, the legislature was unable to agree on legislation in 1854. In 1855, two bills were passed banning the sale (but not manufacture) of liquor, with an exemption for beer and light wine, but the governor vetoed both bills, and the legislature could not muster the votes to override the veto.

To the Hon. Senate and Assembly of Wisconsin.

YOUR undersigned Petitioners, Citizens and Inhabitants of the County of Washington, would respectfully represent to your honorable Bodies, that, for the last three or four years, continuous efforts have been made, on the part of a few organized associations, to legislate upon the virtue of temperance, and to choose the free and sovereign people of this State as the fit subject for their reformatory operations.

Now, the undersigned, as part of this free and self-governing People of Wisconsin, have never, by their free consent, put themselves, their habits, or social relations, under the control or guardianship of temperance or any other set of men. And although it is a source of satisfaction and pleasure to us to see the unfortunate drunkard rise to the dignity of man, we deny to him, if once reformed, the right *therefore* to assume to himself a greater weight in the public affairs than is allotted, in an equal share, to every citizen in this republic. And we do solemnly protest, that our Legislature should be made the stool pigeon for experimental moral reformers, or be regarded as the mere executive of some private associations, bound to carry out by law whatever they, in their private circles, might deign to designate as good and desirable. With the same reason church-going might be enforced by law, or the wholesomest sort of daily food or dress prescribed by law, if certain other private associations should demand such a legislation as promotive of what they conceive a great public good and a great moral reform.

Moral reforms, intending to change some defective habits of the People, should, in the opinion of your Petitioners, be addressed to the People themselves, and carried by an enlightened public opinion,—not by the law and the constable. Laws may make a hypocrite of man, but never a morally better being. Temperance associations, in want of a proper field for their exertions, would do well to turn their attention to a stricter observance of the pledge within their own fold, and not trouble themselves with what kind of habits we might be prone to contract.

The undersigned Petitioners would, therefore, humbly pray your hon[ora]ble bodies, not to abandon this State to the experiments of these one idea fanatics, nor to disagrace the pages of our legislative history by this straggling appendage of the obsolete "blue Laws"—the so-called Maine Liquor Law; but to repeal all those restrictive laws in regard to the regulation of the trade in spirituous liquors, and to leave a reform in this respect with the people themselves. And we will ever pray.[44]

To the Honorable Legislature the Senate and Assembly of Wisconsin.

Your undersigned petitioners—members of the *Muskego Lake Fishing Club*, would respectfully represent, that they have horror struck received the lamentable news that your honorable Bodies are inundated by Petitions for the passage of a Liquor law, similar to that of the state of Maine, and that there is reason to believe you were in favor of such a law.

Now, the undersigned peaceful and industrious Citizens of this State, engaged in the very lawful and respectable business of fishing, would humble remonstrate against such a legislative step, considering it a heavy calamity to the said ancient fishing institution and to the creatures entrusted to their care, for the following weighty reasons:

1. Because they do really believe, that in the case of such law being passed, the dry population, living for 20 miles around the Muskego Lake,

would, in want of any better beverage, take recourse to the water of the said
Lake, in order to quench their thirst, and as water is generally recognised as
a necessary element for the fishes, you are aware that they are in imminent
danger of getting deprived of their first necessity of life, and although our
fundamental laws recognise but the right of *man* to life, yet we dare to
express from the world known benevolent impulses of your noble hearts,
you would magnanimously extend this great right even to the mute beings
entrusted by the scripture to the kind care of the Lord of creation.

2. Because by such a drainage of the Lake, and consequent e[xte]rmi-
nation of the finny tribe, the undersigned company would really be pre-
cluded from the extension of their right to the pursuit of happiness, as
guaranted by our Magna Charta, to every citizen, even to your humble
fishing petitioners.

3. Because fish, in a Baked or fried state of existence, could not swim
but in a distilled or brewed kind of water, there being an old golden rule
of medical diet, that fish in order to be fit for digestion, should swim in
such a liquid.

4. Because it is our custom, well established by a long experience of
our very ancient and respectable order to provide fishes intended for a
long distance, in order to keep them alive, with a sponge in their mouth,
moisted with some, Utard pale or Blossom ale; which we could not do, if
the Maine Liquor law was passed.

5. Because, by passing such a law, intending to multiply the water drinking classes of creation to such an awful extent, your honorable Bodies not
only would deprive this state of such an ornament as our renowned Club,
heretofore has been justly regarded, but you might even put an end to all
water power and to all manufacturing in our dearly beloved Wisconsin.

We need not add that our river improvements, with all the consequent
pleasures of appointing committees, distributing lucrative offices to well
deserving friends, indemnifying contractors etc. would be at an end, and
that, therefore you would be under the necessity to lay an additional bur-
den upon a people, allready grumbling and blinded to the great benefits
of a heavy taxation.

From the above few remarks your honorable Bodies, will, we trust not
fail to arrive to the full conviction that such a legislation as petitioned for
by the friend of the Maine Liquor law, would be extremely prejudice to the

rights of man and beast, and detrimental to your humble petitioners and to the well understood interests of your h[o]n[ora]bl[e] Bodies as well as to those of the whole state. And we hope that you not only will refuse to grant the prayers of those inundating watery petitioners, and refer them to the rest of mankind, but, furthermore, that you would enact the most stringent measures against the adulteration of *Good Liquor*. And we will ever pray.[45]

> In addition to temperance, issues of slavery and race also divided settlers during the era of settlement. Abolitionists in territorial Wisconsin who spoke against slavery did so in peril of their lives. The Reverend Edward Mathews (b. 1812) emigrated to the United States from the United Kingdom in the early 1830s and was appointed a missionary for the Wisconsin Territory by the American Baptist Home Mission Society in 1838. Once in Wisconsin, Mathews embarked upon a ten-year campaign to spread the message of abolition and was one of the founders of the Wisconsin Anti-Slavery Society in 1842. As evidenced by the following entry from Mathews's journal, abolition was not always a popular cause in Wisconsin. Angry mobs—especially in the mining country that had been settled by Southerners—greeted Mathews and his supporters with thrown eggs, taunts, brickbats, and threats of mob violence. Mathews later preached against slavery in Virginia and Kentucky, and in 1851, he returned to the United Kingdom where he continued to speak out against American slavery.

Returning to Mineral Point, I announced that I should preach against slavery on the Sabbath. This the *Miner's Free Press* strongly opposed in a most abusive article. The court house was opened on the Sabbath. The people assembled, and I commenced the meeting. Planks were used for a ceiling above; in the midst of my discourse some of these were removed, and an abundance of eggs were showered down upon me. We adjourned to the outside, and I continued my discourse, being confronted by a large mob. The opponents were armed with clubs, and were led by a stout Irishman. Mr. Martin was severely threatened. In a short time I was interrupted, seized by some of the mob, whose grasp was painful, and dragged into a tavern. At length yielding to my remonstrances, they let me go, and I

Abolitionist Edward Mathews with his "moral map." After returning to the United Kingdom, Mathews lectured in front of a "large moral map . . . in which the slave states were coloured black, and the northern or free states, white." *Monmouthshire Merlin*, August 15, 1855. WHI IMAGE ID 137172

returned to the court house. Many of the mob were standing around Mr. Martin, who requested them to bring forward their members of the bar, or their best informed men, and let them present arguments to show that slavery was right. We, on our part, would prove that it was a sin against God and man. We invited them to try by argument to defend slavery and not rely upon violence.

They were about to seize me again, when a tall, stout New Englander took off his coat, and declared I should be protected. A pro-slavery man then took off his coat, and all began to form into two parties for a contest. Seeing this, rather than that there should be any fighting, I withdrew from the town, uninjured; my clothes, however, bore the impress of the eggs, which it was difficult to remove. . . .

Passing through Fair Play I observed that a neat little Presbyterian chapel had just been built, and it occurred to me that the religious sentiment which led to its erection would be a sufficient protection for me if I lectured on slavery. I made, therefore, an appointment. Before the meeting took place, Mr. Butcher, one of the worst characters in the town, sent me word that if I came there I should be roughly handled by the mob. I thought differently. I went and put up at the house of the Rev. Mr. Dixon, the Presbyterian minister. The place of meeting was crowded, but they were all men. If it was designed to mob a lecturer they usually persuaded the women to stay away. Hence women were termed the Quaker militia—for if they stood between the mob and the lecturer he was safe. In commencing a meeting I would look round, and if I could see a few bonnets, I considered myself out of danger. Mr. Dixon was at my side. We commenced the meeting in the usual mode, by singing and prayer.

I described the sufferings of the slaves at the south, and added, "Such is the condition of our brethren in bonds." Butcher who sat opposite me, whispered a moment to his fellows, then rose and interrupting me said, "Now, sir, before you go any further, you must tell us who you mean by your brethren in bonds!" I wished to reprove him, and to find out how many friends I had in the audience. I responded, "I will take a vote of the audience whether I shall finish the lecture before giving the answer, or answer it now"; and added, "All those who desire me to finish the lecture before replying to the question asked by Mr. Butcher, please to say "Aye." There were a few "Ayes," faintly pronounced. "Now," said Butcher, "all those in favour of my question being answered at once, rise up!" Nearly all the audience sprang to their feet. I thought, I am among my enemies, I will soften down the reply as far as truth will allow, and replied, "All the human family are brethren, because they are all descended from Adam, and these slaves are a part of the human family—therefore, they are brethren." "You mean," said Butcher, "the niggers?" I replied, "The slaves are negroes." He then gave the signal by throwing an egg at me, and the eggs came thick and fast from every part of the room—the mob came prepared and had found a pretext. A brickbat struck Mr. Dixon as he went out. As my cap and overcoat were at the other end of the room I was compelled to wait till the fury of the storm was spent. Butcher then came up and reminded me that he had sent me word that I should be roughly handled if I came there. I told him I had not a particle of unkind feeling against him; I freely forgave him, but I should be glad to ask him one question, "Did not Jesus die for these slaves?" This affected him, and for the moment the sympathy seemed to be turning in my favour. Some, seeing this, proposed further violence, one remarking that my throat ought to be cut. But Butcher restrained them, saying they had gone far enough.

After I arrived at Mr. Dixon's a delegate from the mob made his appearance; he wished to be informed whether I would pledge myself to leave the town by ten o'clock the next morning. I replied that having to lecture twenty-five miles distant the next evening, it would be necessary for me to leave before ten. I supposed there would be no further opposition. But while we were attending family worship we heard a bell ringing in the streets. On rising from our knees, we opened the door, and by the light of the stars could see a black mass approaching the house. "Why," said Mr. Dixon, "here comes the mob." I said, "Send my horse to Jamestown to-morrow morning." Mrs. Dixon was alarmed and said "They will see you—they will see you!" I darted out at the back door and over the fence and ran along the base of the ridge at the bottom of which the town is built; I tried to keep the house, which was detached, between myself and the mob, fearing to ascend the ridge lest I should be seen. But the ravine curved, and as I ran on at its base I looked back, the house did not intercept the view of the mob. I could see them and feared they could see me. My heart sank within me. A thrill of agony ran through my entire system. I thought of the escaping slave pursued by the bloodhounds; but I ran on, and then ventured over the ridge, which now intervened between the mob and myself. I could hear the ringing of the bell, the yells and shouts of the multitude, and the barking of a dog. It seemed to me as if perdition had broken loose.

By the star-light I could see what appeared to be two men, and feared my enemies had tracked me. Stooping down to get a better view, I saw that the figures were rapidly receding from me, and by the sound of their hoofs I discovered that they were horses and not men. This was a great relief. I arrived safely at Jamestown and stayed at the house of a gentleman who would receive me at any time, and the next day my horse was sent to me. I saw Mr Dixon afterwards and inquired what the mob did. "Oh," said he, "they demanded you, and I informed them you were gone to Jamestown. They stated that had you been in my house they would have pulled the house down, unless I had given you up; when they heard that you were an Englishman, they scented for your blood like vultures; and I do not dare pray for the slaves as my brethren in bonds, should I do so they would drive me also from the town."[46]

By the 1840s, the work of men like Mathews began to pay off. Men and women who brought temperance and other ideas of reform from New England also harbored a strong hatred of slavery. Many of them formed anti-slavery societies to rally support for the abolitionist cause. For example, the citizens of Lisbon in Waukesha County, formed an anti-slavery society in early 1844. Their constitution was published in a Milwaukee anti-slavery newspaper, *The American Freeman*, which soon moved to Waukesha County.

Whereas, The most high God has made of one blood all nations to dwell on the face of the earth and established the common brotherhood and equality of mankind: And whereas, our national existence is based upon the great and fundamental principles set forth in the declaration of American Independence—that "all men are created free and equal, and endowed with certain inalienable rights—such as life, liberty and the pursuit of happiness;" and *slavery* being the great antagonist of those rights, inasmuch as it is subversive of those principles of our Holy Religion, violates the rights of humanity, usurps the prerogatives of God, is opposed to the principles of natural justice, to a Republican form of government, is destructive to the prosperity of our country, and hostile to the interest of a civil community. Although confined to certain portions of our land, yet its pernicious influences are felt over the whole body politic, corrupting the moral, social, political, and ecclesiastical relations, thus endangering the peace, union, and liberty of our common country: And whereas, the laws of humanity, the precepts of our Holy Religion, demand its immediate abolition: Therefore, with a firm reliance upon Divine aid, we do hereby form ourselves into an Anti-Slavery Society based upon the following Constitution:

Art. 1st. This society shall be called the Lisbon Anti-Slavery Society.

Art. 2d. The object of this society shall be to free ourselves from all participation in the sin of slavery, and promote the cause of liberty and emancipation throughout our country and the world.

Art. 3d. The means used to promote the object of this society, shall be *free* discussion upon the subject of *Slavery*, the circulation of Anti-slavery tracts, books, papers, &c., and any other measures, moral, political, or religious, we may deem necessary and suitable, *always withholding our suffrages from pro-slavery candidates for office.*

Art. 4th. Any person may become a member of this society by adopting its principles and signing this Constitution.[47]

While white ministers and abolitionists in Wisconsin sought to abolish slavery in the United States, free black Wisconsinites fought against their second-class citizenship in the state. Wisconsin's African American population was still small. In 1840, there were 185 free blacks and 11 enslaved blacks in the territory. By 1850, there were 635 free blacks and no enslaved persons living in Wisconsin. During the territorial and early state eras, Wisconsin limited voting rights to white males, both citizens and noncitizens. Benjamin Hughes of Racine and twelve other African Americans thought that this race barrier was unjust and petitioned the legislature in 1845 to remove color, or race, as a restriction on voting. The legislature defeated a bill the following year, and the territory's voters also rejected black voting rights by a two to one margin in 1847. Eventually, Ezekiel Gillespie, a black man who was turned away at the polls in Milwaukee in 1865, brought a lawsuit, which resulted in a state Supreme Court ruling in 1866 granting African Americans voting rights in the state. That right was reaffirmed four years later when the Fifteenth Amendment to the US Constitution banned voting restrictions based on race or color. While blacks were prohibited from voting, they could make their wishes known by petitioning the legislature. In the following petition, thirteen black residents from Racine gave voice to their desire for equal status at the ballot box.

To the Council and House of Representatives of the Territory of Wisconsin.

[Submitted February 1845]

The undersigned inhabitance of Racine, Racine County, Wisconsin Territory, would respectfuly represent to Your honourable body That while we are bound to observe the *Laws* and *aid* in *main[tain]ing* the Government of this Territory we are nevertheless by existing laws not permitted to exercise the elective franchise on account of our Colour which discrimination we deem unjust oppressive and in violation of the fundamental principles of all republican institutions. We therefore humbly petition Your Honorable body So to amend the laws of this Territory that Colour shall not be the test of the right of Suffrage and as in duty bound we will every pray.

Benj. A. Hughes
William Taylor
David Morgin
James Sweat
Stephen Jefferies
James Galway
Scott Tucker
C. S. Horton
Charles McMullen
J. M. Bell
James Williams
George Williams
William Talbert[48]

On October 7, 1850, a group of African American men met in Milwaukee in response to a new threat to their safety and the safety of other black people in Wisconsin. Passage of the Fugitive Slave Law of 1850, introduced by Senator James Murray Mason of Virginia, mobilized black communities throughout the nation. The law penalized local officials who did not arrest runaway slaves, fined anyone who assisted runaways, denied jury trials to those accused of being runaways, and permitted slave owners to claim a runaway slave by affidavit. The law threatened not only enslaved people who had made their way to free states such as Wisconsin, but also free blacks, who were subject to legalized kidnapping by slave holders.

The black men who met in Milwaukee were well aware of similar groups meeting in New York and Illinois, as mentioned in the document below. At the Milwaukee meeting, several young men delivered speeches in which they described the threat and planned opposition. Although black Milwaukeeans represented a small community of about one hundred in a city of ten thousand, the group that gathered for the meeting agreed that they needed to organize in their defense.

The five speakers whose remarks were printed in the following newspaper article were relatively young and had come from a variety of backgrounds. Lewis Johnson, a thirty-three-year-old barber who had moved from New York, chaired the meeting and warned that the group was facing "Liberty or Death." William Thomas Watson, the twenty-two-year-old son of Sully and Susanna Watson, had moved from Ohio after his father obtained his freedom. Joseph H. Barquet—misspelled Barguet in the newspaper—was a twenty-seven-year-old mason and had been born in the South. Henry Clarke owned his own business—the Pioneer Hair Dressing Salon—and, at thirty-five, was one of the older speakers that evening. Martin Smith worked as a whitewasher. The men adopted resolutions pledging to rescue anyone seized under the Fugitive Slave Law, even at the cost of their lives—and several of the speakers later put their words into action. In 1854, Martin Smith was involved in the efforts to rescue Joshua Glover, whose case led the Wisconsin Supreme Court to become, in 1855, the only state high court in the nation to nullify the law. During

the Civil War, Joseph H. Barquet was a sergeant in the 54th Massachusetts United States Colored Troops, which gained fame for its assault
on Battery Wagner in South Carolina in 1863. The 54th Massachusetts
was later memorialized in the Robert Gould Shaw Memorial in Boston sculpted by Augustus Saint-Gaudens and in the motion picture
Glory. The report of the meeting appeared in the *Milwaukee Daily
Sentinel and Gazette,* October 11, 1850, under the headline "Meeting of
the Colored Citizens of Milwaukee."

At a meeting of the colored citizens of Milwaukee, held Monday evening,
October 7th, Lewis Johnson was appointed Chairman and Joseph H. Barguet, Secretary.

Mr. Johnson, on taking the Chair, acknowledged the honor conferred
on him, and then proceeded to address the meeting, as follows:

Gentlemen: The time has arrived when we are all called upon to do our
duty to ourselves and our God. By the passage of, *a law for the recapture
of fugitive slaves*, entitled "An act to amend and supplementary to the act
of 1793, respecting fugitives from justice and persons escaping from the
service of their masters," which has become the law of the land, we feel
called on to decide for ourselves, whether we will tamely submit to this
enactment, or not. No other alternative is left us but to choose between
Liberty or Death. We are also to say, whether we will suffer our brethren to
be taken back into worse than Egyptian bondage, or whether we will swear
by High Heaven to rescue them at all hazards, even unto death. These are
the questions for you to decide—these are the considerations which have
called you together here to-night. This is the first meeting of any kind in
which the colored people of this State have been called upon to express an
opinion. Illinois has spoken, and the voice of the Empire State has reached
our ears. Though few in number, let us be faithful to ourselves, to our
trembling fugitive brothers, and to our God. Let your resolves be bold—let
them come from the heart, speaking the voice of men who are determined
upon the resolution of Patrick Henry—"Liberty or Death!"

The address of the Chairman was enthusiastically cheered.

On motion of Mr. George H. Clarke, seconded by Mr. Wm. Miner, a
Committee of Five was appointed by the Chair to draft a suitable Preamble

and Resolutions expressive of the sense of the meeting. The Chair appointed Messrs. G. H. Clarke, Alex'r Wilson, W. C. Harlan, John Gardner, and Wm. Miner said Committee.

During the absence of the Committee, Mr. Thos. Watson addressed the meeting, showing the danger of our situation, our liability to be arrested at most any moment, and taken we know not where before we know not whom, and adjudged before any slavish Commissioner or Judge, whose fiat would be omnipotent in deciding us to be chattel property, belonging to any claimant who would commit perjury in swearing to men, women or persons they never saw. In all the bearings of the law, we see no hope, no ray of light, but in self-protection, which is the law of Heaven.

The Secretary, Mr. Barguet, followed.

Gentlemen: From my heart let me pray you to forget every thing like feelings of animosity, forget that you were free-born, forget, you whose parents wore chains, all differences between you; remember only the hour that has arrived when you, one and all, are called on to do your duty to yourselves and your brothers. Springing from one race, let us make common cause, one with another; let us shield one another; let us die for one another. Let us be ready at all times, in all places, whether in security or danger, to throw our lives in the breach when called on; to protect our flying brothers. Remember the slaveholder who seeks to rob him of his all, his life, his liberty, who would rush even unto our hearthstones, and tear from our fond embrace, the children of our loins, yea, the wife of our bosoms. We stand no better chance than the fugitive; and; gentlemen, the blood of Nubia is in our cheeks, the fangs of the blood-hound is not particular as to his prey;—The law is his; Senator Mason has said it; unworthy of the land that gave him birth.

The great charter of human rights, the Habe[a]s Corpus, has been broken down.—Robbed of every right, every protection, save strong arms and brave hearts, what are we to do? Let us, I say, unite; nature teaches us that the wolves hunt in packs to protect themselves. Gentlemen, before you this night, I pledge my life to come forward at any time, and redeem my word; and once more I would add, be ready, sharpen your swords by the midnight lamp, be in the saddle by the first streak of day. If your liberty is worth having, it is worth a life to preserve it. But I am intruding on your time; one word more, and I am done. How heart-sickening it is to reflect upon our situations. We are Americans by birth; the blush of shame comes to my cheek when I think of it, that the land of our nativity refuses us her protection, while she holds out her wide-spread arms to receive a Kossuth, a Paez, Garibaldi, and other fugitives, lovers of Liberty and Republicanism. Let us then, as the last resort, point our brethren to the north star. The eagle no more protects him under the shadow of her wings. Let him go and throw himself under the tender clutches of the British lion. Remember, then, that bayonets may be called upon to uphold such abominations for a time, but surely as the love of freedom swells the hearts of mankind; surely as sweet freedom, once tasted, can never be forgotten, the end of that triumph will be terrible.

The Committee having returned, reported through their chairman, Mr. Clarke, as follows,

Whereas, The Constitution of the United States guarantees its protection to those who shall peaceably meet for all purposes, or to speak of their grievances, and laying their injuries before the people,—and, whereas, a law has been passed by the American Congress, just adjourned, entitled a Bill for the re-capture of Fugitive Slaves, which law we hold to be repugnant to all republican principles of government, trampling under foot every vestige of justice, setting aside the Habeas Corpus and trial by Jury, which have come down to us from the time of the granting of the great Magna Charta; and whereas, the said law gives no protection to bond or free, depriving us of our oaths, leaving no protection, and being thus situated by the passage of this law, we have no other alternative left us but to choose between Liberty or Death; therefore, we, the people of the City and County of Milwaukee, in the State of Wisconsin, do Resolve,

1. That the passage of Mason's Fugitive Bill, is an outrage upon all forms of republicanism, leaving us to choose between Liberty and Death, and that of the alternatives, we choose death to chains.

2. That we pledge ourselves to come forward, at any alarm given, and rescue our fugitive brethren even unto death; further more, that we will stain every inch of earth with our blood for their deliverance, leaving the issue with Israel's God.

3. That as peaceable citizens we respect the laws, but we cannot heed any law that conflicts with the higher law of self-protection—that life, liberty and the pursuit of happiness, are constitutional doctrines we hold

paramount in this case, believing Mason's bloody bill to be antagonistic to those provisions.

4. That our thanks are due to our immediate Senators and Representatives, for their votes against this bloody bill, and also to those noble Senators and Representative from other States, who voted in like manner against it.

5. That the noble Turk who refused to yield up the leaders of Hungarian liberty, as a sacrifice to Russia, has set a noble example worthy of imitation by every lover of justice and liberty in this christen land.

6. That we feel proud of our adopted State, and record, with pleasure, the fact that her hands are clean of the fugitive's blood.

7. That our thanks are also due to those Journals of this City which have opposed the fugitive law, and the remembrance of their aid we will always hold dear.

Mr. Clarke, in offering the Preamble and Resolutions, recommended their adoption. He thought that, in small communities, like ours, we should speak out, and speak boldly and loudly. For we were subject to the inroads or excursions of southern masters. He thought we should echo back the voice of Illinois and the great Empire State. He had, he said, taken no part in politics, but he laid in wait, like the guerilla, to seize his prey; that he never went before the public as a regular, but the time had arrived when all the single bandits have to come into line, for the whole country was in danger—every man to his tent. Mr. C. said he had long resided at the South, and he knew the temerity of some of the "sons of Chivalry." He conceived that this was a plan between the Colonization Society and the late Congress to pass the law, which they thought should frighten us all to Africa, and taken back to Old Virginny, Nullifying South Carolina, or Disunion Georgia, their fugitive brethren. But 'twas all a fancy spell, or the follies of a day. We were to stay here, and protect ourselves, our families, and our brethren. He said we wanted protection, but that protection must only come from ourselves.

Mr. Smith seconded the remarks of Mr. Clarke. He said the time was late, and he should say very little. He felt happy to see the action that had already been taken by the people in other States, upon this momentous question, and felt happier still that Milwaukee had spoken. Though a few in number, they were in action many. He thought the meeting should adopt some signal for their calling forth in time of danger.

The report was accepted, and the Committee discharged. The Resolutions were then separately read and unanimously adopted.

The following letter was received by the Chair, read and ordered to be published with the proceedings:

Milwaukee, Sept. 5th, 1850

Gentlemen. I learn that you are to hold a meeting, on Monday evening; for the purpose of considering the act passed by Congress in relation to the colored people. Permit me to make a few suggestions. We have been grievously wronged—our rights have been taken from us, and we are to take care of ourselves. Now we wish to know the best way to do this. Let us form ourselves into a Society for the mutual protection of each other, and agree, under certain penalties, to live a life that people of all colors will approve. Let all those who will not lead an honorable life be expelled from among us, and we will then have so many friends among the people, that if a whole legion of southerners should come here, they could not take us. I submit this to your consideration. Do with it as you will.

Yours, in the name of Freedom and Justice,

C. D. W.

It was resolved that the proceedings be published in the daily papers of the city.

The meeting then adjourned, subject to the call of the Chair.

Lewis Johnson, Chairman

Jos. H. Barguet, Secretary.[49]

The perception of pioneer Wisconsin as an untamed, violent region with little culture irked many civic-minded residents who wanted to promote the area as a place of opportunity for families. Yet in both fact and fiction, violence played a major role in the settlement of the American West. This excerpt from Juliette Kinzie's memoirs suggests that the administration of justice in early Wisconsin often confirmed stereotypes about the West. She was born Juliette Magill (1806–1870) in Connecticut, and in 1830 she married John Kinzie, a fur trader and Indian agent assigned to Fort Winnebago at Portage, Wisconsin. She traveled across Wisconsin with her husband during the 1830s and gathered stories about early Wisconsin, publishing many of them in her 1856 book *Wau-Bun, the "Early Day" in the North-West*. Although many of these anecdotes are exaggerated, they reflect Kinzie's view of Wisconsin as a rough-and-tumble place during the early nineteenth century. In the following excerpt, Kinzie refers to Charles Reaume, who was a justice of the peace in Green Bay from 1803 until his death around 1821, and Nicholas Boilvin (1761–1827), who had served as a federal Indian agent and as a justice of the peace at Prairie du Chien.

Some instances of the mode of administering justice in those days, I happen to recall.

There was an old Frenchman at "the Bay," named Réaume, excessively ignorant and grasping, although otherwise tolerably good-natured. This man was appointed justice of the peace. Two men once appeared before him, the one as plaintiff, the other as defendant. The justice listened patiently to the complaint of the one, and the defence of the other; then rising, with dignity, he pronounced his decision:

"You are both wrong. You, Bois-vert," to the plaintiff, "you bring me one load of hay; and you, Crèly," to the defendant, "you bring me one load of wood; and now the matter is settled." It does not appear that any exceptions were taken to this verdict.

This anecdote led to another, the scene of which was Prairie du Chien, on the Mississippi.

There was a Frenchman, a justice of the peace, who was universally known by the name of "Col. Boilvin." His office was just without the walls of the fort, and it was much the fashion among the officers to lounge in there of a morning, to find sport for an idle hour, and to take a glass of brandy-and-water with the old gentleman, which he called "taking a little *quelque-chose*."

A soldier, named Fry, had been accused of stealing and killing a calf belonging to M. Rolette, and the constable, a bricklayer of the name of Bell, had been dispatched to arrest the culprit and bring him to trial.

While the gentlemen were making their customary morning visit to the justice, a noise was heard in the entry, and a knock at the door.

"Come in," cried the old gentleman, rising and walking toward the door.

Bell. Here sir, I have brought Fry to you, as you ordered.

Justice. Fry, you great rascal! What for you kill M. Rolette's calf?

Fry. I did not kill M. Rolette's calf.

Justice (shaking his fist). You lie, you great rascal! Bell, take him to jail. Come gentlemen, come, *let us take a leetle quelque-chose....*[50]

Although Kinzie thought these stories were quaint and charming, many Wisconsin residents believed that the territory's future depended on its image as a place of law and order. Boosters of Wisconsin went out of their way to disprove the popular images of the West as an unruly place and tried to show that people and their property were perfectly safe in the state. A good example of this defense of the territory appeared in a Southport (now Kenosha) newspaper in 1841.

It has become extremely fashionable among the newspaper writers at the east, to speak of crime and outrage as a trait of character peculiar to the west. Many eastern journals never speak of the people of the west, only as they would speak of barbarians or a half civilized population.—These traducers of western character are either wilfully ignorant, or maliciously disposed to injure the prosperity of the west. It is through their influence that the more credulous portion of the community at the east, are led to believe that life and property are far less secure here than in New England. Crimes committed in the west commonly receive a more conspicuous notice in eastern papers, and are almost invariably charged to the "morals of the west." The west is continually accused of crimes; offences committed in the west are magnified, which in the states of the east, would be passed by with half the censure which is bestowed upon them. Strangers and emigrants very rarely come among us, who do not express their surprise at the good order which prevails in community, and the respect which is paid to morals. We have heard hundreds express their astonishment at finding so much refinement and intelligence, where they expected the common courtesies and civilities of life, were scarcely observed. Instead of coming into a community of cannibals and violators of law, they find their persons and rights secure and well guarded—instead of finding the sabbath desecrated and unobserved, they find the institutions of religion respected, and a healthful moral influence pervading the state of society—instead of finding the interests of education neglected, they find schools and the means of instruction, keeping pace with our growth in population.

It is true that this gratifying state of society does not exist universally in the west; there are many exceptions; bad men, and bad society, are found in the west as well as in other portions of the United States. But the general aspect of society will not suffer by comparison in point of morals, intelligence, public spirit, and good order, with New England. It is true that crime is committed in the west as well as elsewhere; but that it is of more frequent occurrence, or that the inhabitants have less respect to the majesty of the law than at the east, has no foundation in fact. The progress of crime in the United States it is feared, is rapidly on the increase.—Causes are in operation which are apparently undeveloped, and which appear to escape the detection of human observation; their results are of a startling character, and threaten the destruction of civil society. The newspapers of the day are freighted with chapters of crime of the most appalling nature; the baser passions of mankind seem to be let loose upon the world. Human ingenuity appears to be upon the rack, to seek out new avenues to lawless violence. Man lurks for the blood of his fellow-man, as the beast of prey lies in wait for the victim of his appetite.

But where have recently been committed the most deliberate and atrocious murders? Where have been perpetrated the most daring outrages upon innocence and virtue? Where have been the most studied acts of cold blooded villanny, among those making high pretensions to character and standing in community? Surely not in the west:—Of whatever crimes and iniquities the west may be guilty, and whatever deeds of darkness may have been perpetrated on its soil, none have the enormity of character of those lately committed in the city of New York. Nor is New York alone—other portions of the east have latterly been stained with crimes of a deeper dye than has yet appeared on the catalogue of villiany in Wisconsin or the country in its vicinity. The west, especially the north west, may with justice throw back the foul imputation of crime upon the east. When will the respectable journals of the east throw aside their stereotyped epithets of "crime in the west"—"lawless violence in the west?" Surely the moral sense of the more intelligent portion of community must be tired of this species of libeling.[51]

> While boosters accused Easterners of exaggerating the amount of violence in the West, there were still enough incidents to confirm Wisconsin's rough-and-tumble stereotype. In February 1842, a shooting took place on the floor of the territorial council (the precursor to today's state senate). James R. Vineyard (1804–1863), a Democrat from Grant County, and Charles C. P. Arndt (1811–1842), a Whig from Brown County, clashed over a political appointment. Arndt struck Vineyard in the face, and Vineyard responded by drawing a pistol and shooting Arndt through the heart.
>
> This incident caught the attention of writers on both sides of the Atlantic. British writer Charles Dickens visited America in 1842 and mentioned the shooting in his book *American Notes for General Circulation*. (The following excerpt also makes reference to Dickens's book *The Pickwick Papers* and to his pseudonym, Boz.) This article, written by a Wisconsin correspondent who sat through the trial of Vineyard, appeared in the *New-York Tribune* and confirmed Eastern stereotypes concerning early Wisconsin's legal system. Significant persons mentioned in the essay include defense attorneys Moses Strong (1810–1894), who later served as president of the territorial council and as speaker of the state assembly, and Alexander P. Field (1800–1876), who served as secretary of the territory from 1841 to 1843. It also refers to prosecution witness Ebenezer Brigham (1789–1861), a member of the territorial council.

Wiskonsan—Trial of J. R. Vineyard!

MONROE, (Wis. Ter.)

Oct. 15, 1843.

When I last wrote you, you will recollect I was at Milwaukie. Since then, my course has been still westward, and Thursday night found me at this place, which is the county seat of Green County. The route which I have pursued from Milwaukie here is most beautiful, and the country passed over such as the eye delights to gaze upon. I had heard much of the beauty of the Rock River country, but when I came to survey it myself, I had to acknowledge that "the one half had not been told me."

I crossed Rock River at Janesville, a beautiful and thriving little town with a pretty court house, and what is rare in this country, two elegant and well kept hotels. On arriving here, I found that the court was in session, and that the celebrated case of *the United States v. James R. Vineyard* was about to be brought to trial. Never having been in a Western Court, I had some little curiosity to witness the manner in which the laws are administered in Wiskonsan; and as this case was one that had excited much interest, I thought the present a favorable opportunity. The history of the case is no doubt fresh in your recollection, and is about this: J. R. Vineyard and C. P. Arndt were members of the Legislative Council of the Territory. A dispute arose in the Council Chamber between them. Vineyard charged Arndt with lying; Arndt returned the charge by striking Vineyard with his fist, and Vineyard thereupon drew from his pocket a pistol and shot him dead. The offence was committed at Madison, but a change of venue was taken by the defendant to this county. For some reason or other, the indictment instead of being for murder, was simply for manslaughter, and upon that charge he was tried here.

The Jury, as finally settled, presented an interesting group I assure you, and it would be no figure of speech to say that such another could not be obtained this side of Botany Bay. I noticed that the defendant managed to reject every man from the Jury who presented any outward appearance of intelligence. You have read Pickwick, and must recollect the intelligent Jury in the noted case of Bardell vs. Pickwick. Just turn to the inimitable illustration of that Jury by "Phiz," and you have a perfect fac simile of the intelligence of the Jury that tried Vinyard.

The examination of witnesses occupied an entire day, and many were examined on both sides, principally on the part of the defendant to show that he acted in self defence. Witnesses were, however, examined who proved the previous good character of the accused, and that he was uniformly considered a kind and humane man.

After the closing of the evidence, the case was opened by the Prosecuting Attorney for the county, but I think I have heard James R. Whiting display greater ability on similar occasions. The prosecution was followed on the part of the defence by a man by the name of Strong, who I understood

The 1837 illustration by Phiz (Hablot K. Browne) from *The Pickwick Papers* by Charles Dickens. This is the illustration mentioned on page 144.

lived somewhere over near the Mississippi, in the Mining Country, in a speech of about three hours in length, and *such* a speech, I guess, was never made before or since upon such an occasion. I would like to give you an idea of it, but it would be hardly possible. Before commencing he had a pitcher of Whiskey brought into the Court room, and set on the table before him, from which he drank long and frequently, so frequently that before he got half through with his speech he "reeled to an fro, and staggered like a drunken man." He commenced by telling the Jury what an intelligent, high-minded, and honorable set of men they were, giving them first a compliment all round; then after going through with a detail of the case, he selected out one juryman, whose name was Rutledge, (one, who, when examined as to his qualifications for a juror, said he could neither read nor write,) and addressed him about thus: "And you, Mr. Rutledge, I cannot pass you by. You remind me of your noble ancestor, Edward Rutledge of South Carolina; him who signed the Declaration of Independence. What would your noble ancestor have done had he been assailed as Vineyard was, in the Hall of Independence? would he not have done as Vineyard did? Would not you have done the same under like circumstances? I know you would, I know you are not the man to stain the glory of your worthy progenitor." And then, after going on a while, and saying a great deal that had just about as much to do with the trial of Vineyard as the man in the moon, he says, "Gentlemen of the Jury, I dont know what your religion is, nor I dont care, I haint got much myself, though Jesus Christ was a mighty good man. Now, gentlemen, I am one of those kind of men who live pretty fast. I believe men generally live over about the same surface: some live long and narrow, and others live broad and short.

I am one of the kind who live broad and short. I sometimes dread lest I should live to be old. I would not like to live to be as old as that man Brigham (alluding to a witness who was a member of the Council at the time of the difficulty, and who told a very strait and clear story) lest I should become forgetful like him. As to that other old gentleman who looked so sleek, I don't mean to say that he testified falsely, but that he was mistaken. I would not like to charge him with perjuring himself because he and I were members of the Council together. We were tolerable good friends, though always quarreling. He was always on one side; he was just like the handle of this pitcher, (taking up the pitcher and pointing to the handle,) here, gentlemen, this was him, and here (pointing to the nose of the pitcher) this was the estimable Moses, and these were our relative positions. I believe we never got so near as to drink a glass of water together, but I'll drink his health now any how" (catching up the pitcher and pouring down a strangler of whiskey.) When he came to speak of Arndt, the unfortunate man who was slain by Vineyard, it was about in this strain: "Arndt, gentlemen, is dead;

there is no doubt of it. he is dead! dead! dead as a smelt; in the language of Tippecanoe and Tyler too, he is 'a gone coon.'" Then, after branching out in a long tirade of abuse of old England and the laws which we have adopted from her, he remarked, that he knew very well that if he were making that speech in Vermont, he would get rowed up Salt-River high and dry, but before a jury in Green County he thought it would do,—at all events he would risk it. After speaking about two hours he wanted to bring his speech to a close, but he had then got so completely drunk that he could not, but had to go on speaking and repeating what he had before said for an hour longer, but he finally succeeded in winding up and the Court adjourned to the next morning. Had I left after hearing that speech and witnessing the monkey-shines of the speaker, without hearing the concluding Counsel for the prosecution and defence, I should have been constrained to believe that all I had previously heard of western courts of justice was true, but the concluding argument for the defence, which was made by Col. Field, the Secretary of the Territory, was dignified, able, and suited to the occasion, as was also the closing argument for the prosecution made by Mr. Collins of Madison. The judge (who by the way is about forty years of age and much of a gentleman in appearance) charged the jury very handsomely and impartially for about fifteen minutes, they then retired and after a short absence returned a verdict of *"Not Guilty"* Thus farcically has terminated this celebrated case,—one of the cases that was considered of sufficient note by Boz, to be noted down in his "Notes for General Circulation." The accused is a man below the middling size, about forty years of age, and of rather gentlemanly deportment, and is said to have a great many personal friends in the county of his residence, all of which is no doubt true, which fact in this country may afford a sufficient justification of the act committed, but I reckon it would hardly do in your State, or any other law-loving community. I shall leave here to-morrow for Galena, the great Lead Mart of the Mining Country, from which place you shall hear from me again.

Yours, &c.

E.G.B.[52]

Territorial newspapers, conscious of the impact of the Arndt-Vineyard affair, looked for ways to reduce the territory's dangerous image, as evidenced in this editorial entitled, "The Practice of Carrying Deadly

Weapons," from a Madison newspaper. The paper's editor appealed to the public, stating that armed men should be shunned and asking if the carrying of weapons should be outlawed. The Wisconsin legislature did not act on the newspaper's proposal.

In our remarks last week upon the horrid tragedy which had just transpired in the Capitol, we alluded to the practice of carrying fire arms or other deadly weapons, and promised some further remarks upon that subject next week.

We are aware that in some parts of the country this practice is very common, so much so that deadly weapons are considered an essential part of the equipage of a *gentleman*. If by the term *gentleman* we are to understand, a man who can without remorse and without a blush, shoot or stab his neighbor to the heart, for some trifling affront, real or imaginary, there may be some appropriateness of the practice to the character. But whatever may be the sentiment of other portions of the country, we do sincerely hope that the moral sense of the people of this Territory will attach a different meaning to the term.

In other days, and in other parts of the world, the time has been when personal safety depended upon the possession of the means necessary for a successful resistance of personal aggressions, in a personal manner. This indeed may be necessary in a rude, uncivilized anarchical state of human society, where LAW has never been enthroned, where every man's house is his fortress, and the preservation of his common rights depends upon the strength of his own right arm. Such a state of society, however, when we reflect seriously upon its elements, we shall find destitute of every thing lovely and desirable, and fraught beyond endurance with all that is fearful in tendency, and revolting and odious in character. Who would be willing to exchange, as the means of his personal safety, the prisons and fortresses of his country, for the miserable defence which he might be able to throw around his own dwelling? Who would be willing as a means of defending his rights and redressing his wrongs, to exchange the organized force and strong arm of a law-abiding nation for a dirk and a pocket pistol? Who, we ask, even for a large share in the rapine and plunder inseparable from such a state of society, would be willing to run such fearful hazards? And again we ask, *who?* Is there no answer? Yes, there is. The man—the *gentleman?*—

the man who struts about in society, affecting to be above the restraints and independent of the protection of law, and placing his confidence in his blade and firelock, answers AYE, and calls himself a man of HONOR! There are quite too many of these honorable worthies in our country, more by far than the *less honorable* portion of the community are aware of; and however they may endeavor to perfume themselves with the name of honor, they cannot but be regarded by all good citizens as the enemies of mankind and opposed to the restraints of all law, human and divine.

In a country like ours, where a perfect and efficient system of law throws its ample protection over and around every citizen, there can be no excuse for a practice so fraught with danger to society, and which could only be justified by the prevalence of downright anarchy, and the absence of all other means of defence; and we wonder it should be tolerated in any civilized community. It cannot be supposed that a man would carry these instruments of death about his person, without an intention to use them. No man would submit to the *inconvenience* of carrying in his pocket a pistol or a dagger, without some motive; and the very fact that a man carries these weapons about him, is evidence to some extent at least, that he intends to take the law into his own hands, or rather to trample it under his feet; and every such man *should be regarded as a mob,* on a small scale it is true, but at the same time of the most dangerous character.

Mobs of any kind, whether single-handed or in congregated masses, and for any ostensible purpose, cannot but be inconceivably ruinous to the best interests of society; all having the same tendency to dethrone law, and establish in its place the wild rule of passion. The outrages which have been committed within the past few years by the growing spirit of mobocracy in this country, have justly excited fear and alarm in the minds of all reflecting men; and it matters not whether a mob be directed against the Abolitionists, the Banks, the Mormons, or any thing else, good, bad or indifferent, its tendency is substantially the same, the subversion of all law and the sacrifice of every right of man upon the altar of violence. If we admit the propriety of a mob in any case or for any cause whatever, we that moment repudiate all law, and surrender every right; for there is no resting point between the supreme authority of *Law,* and the absolute reign of *Terror*—between that state of society in which no act of violence can go unpunished, and that in which men may with impunity be butchered in the streets, in their houses, or in the capitol of their country. *There is no alternative*—WE MUST ABIDE BY LAW, or WE MUST SUBMIT TO ANARCHY.

This is a maxim which the American people are slow to receive; but receive it we must sooner or later, though it may be taught us by sorry experience.

An important question is, what can be done to prevent the practice to which we have alluded? We are aware that constitutional objections might be raised against a law prohibiting the carrying of deadly weapons, even on ordinary occasions. How far such objections might be valid, we cannot tell; but it does appear to us that laws are passed at almost every session of our legislature, which are far more objectionable in this respect than such an one would be.

Whether such a law if passed would prove efficient is also a question; but one thing appears to us certain, that the common law which palliates and even changes the character of an act when committed under the influence of momentary passion, might be so strengthened by legislation as to neutralize the palliating circumstances in all cases of crime committed by means of such weapons. It seems highly improper that a man should be allowed to go prepared, weeks and months beforehand, for the commission of an outrage, and then because the final act was committed in a moment of excitement, be excused on the ground that it was done without forethought.

The very fact of a man having kept himself in a state of constant readiness for the commission of a crime, without regard to any particular victim, but to kill any man who should offer what he might consider sufficient insult; we say that this very fact ought to be regarded as the strongest evidence of *malice prepense*. But while we would urge this subject upon the consideration of legislators, we would also say that public sentiment should most unequivocally condemn and discountenance this dastardly, and worse than savage practice. Let every man who carries deadly weapons, whatever may be his outward show, be looked upon with suspicion and shunned as a viper.[53]

Politics in early Wisconsin, like the administration of justice, was often informal and rowdy. Candidates for office vilified their opponents in campaign speeches and freely swayed voters with beer and whiskey. Victory celebrations, like the campaigns themselves, were frequently loud and boisterous. Christian Traugott Ficker warned potential immigrants about them in his German-language guide for immigrants. (For background on Ficker and his guide, see pages 8–9.)

The election of representatives is by direct vote of the people. There are definite days in the year in which the male members of every precinct over twenty-one years of age come together at a designated place and there give their votes for that one or those deemed most suited to the offices in question. It cannot be otherwise than that very shameful things happen among a free people in connection with these matters, when men try to build up for themselves a profitable office. Money and particularly intoxicating liquors of all kinds are used in the election at the expense of such office seekers, and not infrequently they attain their goal through them, since there are enough people who are willing to sell their honor, their freedom, and their vote for a glass of wine, beer, or whiskey. In this neighborhood where many educated men live who look upon such doings with disgust, they have begun to set a term to this disgraceful business and there is more than one example of a candidate who has expended hundreds in order to secure a given office, which nevertheless he failed to receive.

Candidates themselves often belittle one another. They bring to light everything that they know to one another's discredit, so that one would suppose they would never look at one another again. But herein one is greatly mistaken, bon honneur does not reach that far among these gents. An amusing incident of this kind which I personally saw and heard I cannot withhold from my readers. I once came back from a visit on election day. As I neared Grafton, I saw a crowd of men standing in front of a house and two gentlemen of Cedarburg, both of whom I knew well, getting into their carriage to drive together, probably homeward. Both were candidates for one and the same office. Hardly had they driven ten steps from the house when one of them pulled up the horse, gave the lines into the hands of the other, stood up and belabored his associate in a manner which it is impossible for me to describe. He naturally built himself up in every way.

The other sat quietly beside him and did not even sulk. Now the first one was through and took over the lines again to drive away. The vehicle had hardly moved a couple of steps from the place when the second one grabbed the lines, stopped, stood up, and in the most impertinent manner delivered himself against the first-named, meanwhile praising himself naturally as the honest James. Having turned his heart inside out, they both drove off harmoniously together. I leave it to each of my readers to make his own comment upon these doings. I at least know that it gave me a feeling of nausea and of the profoundest disgust.

If the office to be filled is an important one, the victorious party raises an indescribable jubilation and often manifests its joy over victory through the wildest doings. For example, in the year 1848 when I was first in Milwaukee for a few days and stood in the evening with a certain Mr. Weber of Chemnitz before the door of our living quarters, the heavens reddened and we certainly thought that a fire had broken out in the city. The landlord, however, said to us it was probably a victory bonfire. Since we did not know what this might be, we went through the alley until we heard a tremendous shouting and finally came to the source of it. Here in the middle of a cross street were some three or four cords of wood piled up and fired, and the youngsters, who above all were most occupied with the matter, were constantly carrying boxes, chests, etc., which (as we were told) the merchants had set out from their stores for this purpose, and were throwing these into the flames which already reached almost to the gables of the houses. Such a crazy, childish, and even highly dangerous rejoicing had never come to our knowledge before. It is however, quite customary, particularly in American cities.[54]

> The partisan bickering described by Ficker in the previous piece did not end once the election was over. Conflict between the legislature and the governor is evident in this letter from Charles Minton Baker to his wife, Martha. (For background on Baker, see pages 21–22.) Baker was a Democratic member of the territorial council (the precursor to today's state senate) from 1842 to 1846. The wild world of early Wisconsin politics was by no means restricted to the campaign stump, and Baker held back nothing in his vivid description of Wisconsin Governor James Duane Doty (1799–1865).

Charles Minton Baker. WHI IMAGE ID 105839

Madison, March 12, 1843

My dear Martha,

I arrived here on Saturday, the day after I left home, having suffered somewhat from the severity of the cold. I came near losing the boarding place I had engaged when here in Dec., another member having taken my place at the adjourned session in Jan'y., but I finally succeeded in getting in under a modified arrangement. I have very comfortable quarters in a pleasant, accomodating & pious family & we live well & every thing is neat. We have eight members of the Legislature who board at the same house with myself. They are sociable & agreeable & most of them are professors of religion. So you see that on the whole I am as comfortably & pleasantly situated as I well could be any where away from home; but after all "there is no place like home". My health has been tolerable tho' I have been troubled somewhat with the dyspepsia. I have to be rather careful in my diet. Altho' there is much for me to do in the discharge of my duties as a member of the Legislature, yet I do not find it any thing like so harrassing & exhausting as attending courts; for here, when I feel unwell I can keep my room & recruit. With a little prudence I think I can enjoy about as good health here as at home.

As to our Legislative affairs, we are very unpleasantly situated owing to the crooked, perverse & reckless course the governor pursues. From personal observation I believe him to be a double-dealing, crafty, short-sighted, dishonest man, destitute alike of sound judgment & sound morals. I can not give you a detail of all his serpentine course the few days we have been here, nor would you be interested to hear it. Suffice it to say he first hesitated to meet us, then sent in his message recognizing us in full; then threatened to dissolve us because we were met under the adjournment, then returned a bill sent to him for his approval waiving that objection but with two other new objections which he had just discovered. The bill is passed unanimously without him, excepting one vote; & now he officially demands of the members of the council their *private* reasons for coming up here, & tomorrow or next day I have no doubt he will refuse to hold any communication with us. So we are in uncertainty & a jangle the whole time & shall probably be unable to do much this session. I think we shall adjourn & go home at the end of 20 days without having effected anything of importance.

I have just returned from hearing a discourse from Rev. Mr. Clark, the resident minister at this place, delivered in the Council Hall which is used as a place of worship. It was extremely well written & appropriately delivered. A large number of the members of both Houses were present. About one fourth of both houses are professors of religion. But there are very few church members resident in Madison. This place much needs a healthy moral & religious influence.

How happy should I be could I this evening be at home in the bosom of my dear family away from the turmoil & excitement which here prevails. I feel that I love you all more than I dare express & may God preserve & bless you. I send you & Mary my love with a kiss. Tell Charles I hope & expect he will be a good boy, obey his mama & behave himself like a man. Say to Edward it will please me very much if I find on my return that he has improved in reading & spelling. Kiss Robert for me & tell him that if he will learn all his letters before papa comes home, I will buy him a present. . . .

Yours most affectionately

Charles[55]

Hundreds of thousands of pioneers traveled to Wisconsin to build new lives for themselves between the mid-1830s and 1850s. They came with differing backgrounds, customs, and assumptions, as well as a variety of personal temperaments. They looked for work, established farms, married, and set up households while struggling with issues of cultural retention and change. Collectively, they argued about and decided what laws, moral standards, and customs would prevail in their new state. They faced public issues such as alcohol abuse, slavery and racial inequity, violence, government regulation, and the justice system among many others. In the process, they built lives and families, as well as institutions, customs, and traditions that we have inherited. Together, they made Wisconsin.

Epilogue

"A MORE FRIENDLY, NEIGHBORLY FEELING"

Reflections on Wisconsin's Identity

During its first decade of statehood, Wisconsin shook off its pioneer image and began to take its place among the more established states in the Union, as local governments, churches, schools, and cultural organizations were founded and flourished. Regions farther west than Wisconsin came to be considered "the rugged West," which had always been more of a concept than a physical place. During Wisconsin's pioneer era, as people flowed into its small but growing towns and as new communities of settlers blossomed all over the countryside, a distinct state identity began to emerge. A place that had once been the exclusive home of American Indian nations, then a contested colonial prize for distant European powers, and finally part of something called the Northwest Territory materialized into a state in the federal union.

Only a dozen years after achieving statehood, the settlers of Wisconsin identified with the Union and sent troops fighting for its cause into the Civil War. No longer simply the name of a river, Wisconsin became both a political entity and also a place with its own cultural identity. Although today this identity is often taken for granted, early residents participated in its creation, and they often contemplated Wisconsin's past, its future prospects, and its very nature and essence. The following three pieces demonstrate how some pioneers viewed this place we now call Wisconsin. Writing prior to statehood, each essayist reflects on a different characteristic of Wisconsin. The first, written in 1838, looks toward the future with boundless optimism. The second, written in 1847, looks to the past and marvels at the territory's amazing changes. The final essay, from 1844, tries to describe the "Wisconsin Character." The theme running throughout is a self-conscious awareness of living through a historic period of change.

The following excerpt from an anonymous essay, which appeared in the *Miners' Free Press* of Mineral Point in 1838, reflects the commonly held belief of many early residents that Wisconsin's prospects as a future state were virtually unlimited.

Our beautiful, interesting, and fertile country is beginning to awake in the minds of the people of the eastern States a lively sensation; it is rapidly growing into importance, and is destined, at no distant day, to shine as brightly as any of the sister States that comprise our Union. The evidence of this, is its rapidly increasing population, which its valuable mineral productions, its excellent soil, the many superior business locations which are to be found on its navigable waters, and last, though not least, its healthful and salubrious climate. These are all powerful attractions, and must have their due weight and influence upon those who turn their attention to the west. All that is necessary to render this country of the first consequence, is to have it well filled with an intelligent, enterprising, and sturdy population; those who are already here, are exclusively of that class. Here, where but eight or ten years since the white man first set his foot—here, where the aborigines of the country in their primitive state roamed over plain, hill, and valley, in search of the deer, or their enemy—here, where hunting, fishing, and war were the only occupations of the red man—are now seen beautiful farms, yielding to the husbandman a rich harvest—the sod is removed and the earth gives to the digger her valuable minerals; with the first dawn of day is heard the sound of the anvil, and the teamster's cry to his sluggish though faithful oxen, the stir and hum of a busy and thriving population. We would invite all who have a wish to remove to the west, to wend their way here; there is plenty of room; all that is desirable is to have it filled. No man need fear. The farmer can find a farm to please—the mechanic a shop with plenty of customers, and the laborer plenty to do, at high wages. The capitalist here can invest his money safely, and that, too, at a good interest. We do not believe there is a country on earth that combines so many advantages as this. In a few years more, Wisconsin will be a State; she will have her seminaries of learning, her rail roads, and her canals, and a population unsurpassed in intelligence, enterprise, and devotion to the best interests of their country and its institutions.[56]

> While looking to the future, many of Wisconsin's residents, even on the eve of statehood, were beginning to reflect upon the territory's past. In 1846, two years before statehood was granted, a number of the territory's citizens formed the Wisconsin Historical Society. A year later, in a speech to the Milwaukee Common Council, Mayor Solomon Juneau (1793–1856) reflected on the city's history. In 1819, Juneau moved to a small trading post on the Menominee River, and a few years later, he built the first house in what is now Milwaukee. By 1835, Juneau began selling lots to settlers in his new town, and he remained an important figure in Milwaukee's early history. In 1846, he was elected the first mayor of Milwaukee, and after serving one term he gave the following speech contemplating the city's explosive growth during his lifetime.

GENTLEMEN—

Before I vacate the chair, I wish to make a few remarks to your Honorable Body.

When I first set foot on this soil some thirty years ago, I little thought that during my age and generation, I should behold such a sight as now presents itself.

Then the red man was supreme monarch of the place on which our delightful city now stands; the plains and the rivers of Wisconsin belonged to him and were subject to his wild control, but now the scene has changed, the war whoop of the Indian has given way to the mild councils of civilized and intelligent men: the wigwam is supplanted by massive and ornamental structures: the place of the bark canoe, which was then the only craft that floated upon the waters of the noble river that meanders through the heart of your city, has been filled by the hundreds of vessels propelled by

Solomon Juneau, first mayor of Milwaukee. WHI IMAGE ID 9483

steam and wind, that now annually visit our shores and enter our harbor, laden with the commerce of the east, and bear off the surplus produce of Wisconsin.

Here we behold a city of twelve thousand inhabitants, with her beautiful streets and walks, her fine gardens and splendid buildings and her intelligent and enterprising population, when eleven years since the soil was unbroken.

I have been a resident of your city from its first commencement to the present day, and trust gentlemen, you will do me the justice to believe that its interest, growth, and prosperity have ever been, and still are, my dearest desire; that it may continue to increase in size and population is my sincere wish. That we may have wholesome laws, and the same well administered will be my earnest prayer when I shall have retired from the honorable and responsible station to which the partiality of my fellow citizens has elevated me.[57]

> As new arrivals from America and Europe began to flood into Wisconsin between the mid-1830s and the 1850s, many residents considered the area's new human resources as promising as its material wealth. In the following editorial from the *Racine Advocate*, the author argues that certain intangible aspects of the prospective state are just as important to its future as its natural resources. The article shows how Wisconsin changed the people who moved there. It celebrates the opportunity to mix with settlers from other states and nations, resulting in new attitudes, ideas, and way of doing things. Wisconsin's pioneers soon became marked by self-reliance, a good work ethic, and public spiritedness. Finally, Wisconsin was marked by "a more friendly, neighborly feeling" in which "all take an interest in the welfare of each and of all together." Combined, these were the elements that made the "Wisconsin Character."

Wisconsin Character

We stated in a former article, that the emigration of the present day consisted largely of the young, the enterprising, and the intelligent. There are other causes which are indeed more or less incident to the settlement of every new country, continually in operation here to develope the noblest traits of the human character. We shall endeavor cursorily to point out a few of these—more with the hope of awakening the attention of some more profound observer to the subject, than with the expectation of doing it justice.

We remark, in the first place, that a residence in a new country is peculiarly favorable to freedom and independence of mind. The emigrant leaves all his acquaintances, friends and relations, and, settles among strangers. He is thrown at once into entirely different circumstances and associations; he has no one to lean upon for influence, assistance or advice, but must rely entirely upon himself. What nobler virtue is there than self-reliance? He must select a farm for himself, he must lay it out, plan the buildings, and in fact do all except what nature has done. How different this is from living in the house and cultivating the farm which his fathers have occupied before him! Perhaps his location is remote from neighbors, or mechanics, or stores; if so, he resorts to a thousand new expedients, and contrives to be entirely independent of the rest of the world. This gives full scope and variety of play to all his physical and mental powers. The extreme division of labor, as practised in the more civilized communities, tends powerfully to contract the mind. What can be more injurious to character, then to be employed in a factory, or in making pin heads all one's life? That a love of freedom and independence are the marked characteristics of the settlers of every new country, is illustrated by the early history of every State in the Union. Indeed this cause alone has had more influence than all other causes in securing to us a free government.

A residence in a new country awakens enterprise. Our citizens, as a general thing, are more industrious than those of any other portion of the country, not even excepting rocky New England. Why? Because they have greater inducements for exertion. A farmer in the older States with but little capital may toil incessantly, and by his economy deprive himself of most of the comforts of life, yet make but little or nothing more than a bare support for himself and family, and all the while be considered of no account in society. How discouraging his situation! Can he work with good heart? Let him come here, and what a new scene bursts upon him. He sees within his reach not only competence, but wealth, and immediately with high hopes endeavors to attain them.

It calls for the public spirit. The resident of the new country sees clearly that the value of his own property depends upon the progress and improvement of the whole country. He takes a warm interest in establishing and improving roads. He contributes liberally to the support of schools and churches. In short, every enterprise which is for the public good, meets with far greater support in a new country than in an old. There is a more friendly, neighborly feeling prevailing; all take an interest in the welfare of each and of all together. This sentiment of public spirit is nearly allied to patriotism, and is far more liberalizing and ennobling than an exclusive devotion to one's immediate interest.

The people in one of the old agricultural towns of New England have all nearly the same habits, manners, ideas and religion; few changes are made in their society from year to year. They live where their fathers did and as their fathers did, and have numerous relations about them in every direction. The settler here finds within the limits of his acquaintance people from all the northern States and from many foreign countries, and those, too, who have formerly been engaged in a variety of occupations different from his own; consequently, he acquires a great variety of new ideas, and becomes much more liberal in all his opinions and views of life.

If one's own improvement is the great object of life, and if independence of mind, originality of thought, self-reliance, enterprise, public spirit, and liberality of opinion are among the highest and noblest of virtues; and a life here is peculiarly calculated to elicit and cultivate all these in addition to all our advantages of health, society, laws and pecuniary prospects, what place can offer greater inducements to emigrants than Wisconsin?[58]

—||—

Some experiences of Wisconsin's pioneers—moving to a new place, getting married, or starting a new job—may feel familiar to the twenty-first-century reader. Other experiences described by early settlers in this book—such as fighting to abolish slavery or to ban alcohol—may be more difficult to relate to, though attitudes about politics or worries about violence may be more recognizable. In the documents excerpted here, men and women who created new lives and new institutions nearly two centuries ago tell us not only about themselves, but also about our lives in modern-day America. Many of their concerns are long gone, and some of their assumptions about race, gender, and ethnicity seem odd or even repugnant today. Yet by reading their words, learning about their triumphs and defeats, and sharing in their joys and anxieties, we come to understand more about our own lives. Rather than encountering stern, dour people whose images are frozen in time, the voices captured in this book provide us with an opportunity to meet, if only briefly, people from the past who had strong emotions and feelings. The exuberance and excitement of pioneers, as well as their loneliness and discouragement, are not unfamiliar to us. As we try to build our own lives and our own communities, we can take some comfort knowing that others have trod similar paths before us.

Notes

1. Alice E. Smith, *From Exploration to Statehood*, The History of Wisconsin, Vol. 1, ed. William Fletcher Thompson (Madison: State Historical Society of Wisconsin, 1973), 466; Richard N. Current, *The Civil War Era, 1848–1873*, The History of Wisconsin, Vol. 2, ed. William Fletcher Thompson (Madison: State Historical Society of Wisconsin, 1976), 76.

2. Caleb Atwater, *Remarks Made on a Tour to Prairie du Chien; Thence to Washington City, in 1829* (Columbus, Ohio: Jenkins and Grover, 1831), 121–122.

3. *The Southport Telegraph*, October 20, 1840.

4. *The Wisconsin Magazine of History* 25 (1941–1942): 471–474.

5. The Henry S. Eggleston Papers, Wisconsin Historical Society Archives.

6. *Proceedings of the State Historical Society of Wisconsin at its Fifty-Ninth Meeting Held October 26, 1911* (Madison: State Historical Society of Wisconsin, 1912), 188–200.

7. *The Wisconsin Magazine of History* 5 (1921–1922): 391–401.

8. *The Wisconsin Magazine of History* 5 (1921–1922): 401–403.

9. *The Wisconsin Magazine of History* 21 (1937–1938): 68–71, 82.

10. *The Wisconsin Magazine of History* 29 (1945–1946): 207–220.

11. *Wisconsin Historical Collections* 15 (1900): 301–303, 306–309.

12. *The Wisconsin Magazine of History* 25 (1941–1942): 224–226.

13. *Wisconsin Historical Collections* 15 (1900): 323, 325–326, 330–331, 333.

14. *The Wisconsin Magazine of History* 7 (1923–1924): 355–363.

15. The John Hodgson Collection, Wisconsin Historical Society Archives.

16. *The Wisconsin Magazine of History* 25 (1941–1942): 332–333.

17. Milo M. Quaife, ed., *An English Settler in Pioneer Wisconsin: The Letters of Edwin Bottomley, 1842–1850* (Madison: State Historical Society of Wisconsin, 1918), 35–36, 39.

18. *The Mineral Point Miners' Free Press*, November 16, 1839.

19. Theodore Christian Blegen, ed., *Land of Their Choice: The Immigrants Write Home* (Minneapolis: University of Minnesota Press, 1955), 75, 78–79.

20. Quaife, *An English Settler*, 67.

21. Quaife, *An English Settler*, 210–214.

22. The Joseph M. Street Papers, Wisconsin Historical Society Archives.

23. *Wisconsin Historical Collections* 15 (1900): 209.

24. The Irwin Family Papers, Wisconsin Historical Society Archives.

25. The Racheline S. Wood Papers, Wisconsin Historical Society Archives.

26. *The Wisconsin Magazine of History* 16 (1932–1933): 89–91, 93–94, 199–200, 202.

27. *Chilton Times Journal*, June 14, 1884.

28. Wisconsin Legislature, Petitions, Remonstrances, and Resolutions, 1842, Wisconsin Historical Society Archives.

29. Blegen, *Land of Their Choice*, 183–187.

30. Gunnar J. Malmin, trans. and ed., *America in the Forties: The Letters of Ole Munch Ræder* (Minneapolis: University of Minnesota Press for the Norwegian-American Historical Association, 1929), 65–69.

31. Quaife, *An English Settler*, 148–149.

32. Harry H. Anderson, ed., *German-American Pioneers in Wisconsin and Michigan: The Frank-Kerler Letters, 1849–1864* (Milwaukee: Milwaukee County Historical Society, 1971), 77, 82.

33. *The Wisconsin Magazine of History* 50 (1966–1967): 256–259.

34. *The Wisconsin Magazine of History* 18 (1934–1935): 331–336.

35. *The Wisconsin Magazine of History* 15 (1931–1932): 359–363.

36. *The Wisconsin Magazine of History* 25 (1941–1942): 228–231, 334–336.

37. *The Wisconsin Magazine of History* 7 (1923–1924): 363–368.

38. Anderson, *German-American Pioneers*, 71, 72.

39. Anderson, *German-American Pioneers*, 155–158.

40. Malmin, *America in the Forties*, 15–19, 37–43.

41. *The Revivalist*, January 8, 1834.

42. *The Revivalist*, January 22, 1834.

43. The American Home Missionary Society Papers, Wisconsin Historical Society Archives.

44. Wisconsin Legislature, Petitions, Remonstrances, and Resolutions, 1852, Wisconsin Historical Society Archives.

45. Ibid.

46. *The Wisconsin Magazine of History* 52 (1968–1969): 128–129, 249–250.

47. *The American Freeman*, March 27, 1844.

48. Wisconsin Legislature, Petitions, Remonstrances, and Resolutions, 1845, Wisconsin Historical Society Archives.

49. "Meeting of the Colored Citizens of Milwaukee," *Milwaukee Daily Sentinel and Gazette,* October 11, 1850.

50. Mrs. John H. Kinzie, *Wau-Bun, the "Early Day" in the North-West* (New York: Derby & Jackson, 1856), 45–46.

51. *The Southport Telegraph,* October 26, 1841.

52. *The New-York Tribune,* November 4, 1843.

53. *The Wisconsin Enquirer,* February 23, 1842.

54. *The Wisconsin Magazine of History* 25 (1941–1942): 457–459.

55. Edward Larrabee Baker, *Charles Minton Baker and the Pioneer Trail* (Chicago: privately printed, 1928), 278–280.

56. *The Miners' Free Press,* August 7, 1838.

57. *Milwaukee Sentinel and Gazette,* April 15, 1847.

58. *The Racine Advocate,* March 5, 1844.

INDEX

Note: Page numbers in *italics* denote illustrations. Locations are in Wisconsin unless otherwise noted.

children: bilingual abilities of, 82, 116; clothing of, 77; diary of, 16–21; and farm life, 9, 90; illnesses of, 32, 37–38, 59, 60; parents' love and hopes for, 82, 85, 86, 108; schools for, 68–69, 72, 98, 118–120; ship travel with, 27, 29, 31, 32, 36, 37–38

Chippewa (tribe). *See* Ojibwe (tribe)

churches. *See* religions

Clark, Rev., 154

Clarke, Henry, 134–139

climate: fall, 52; general, 6; spring, 52–53; storms, xi, 27, 31, 34, 36, 38, 54, 85, 107; summer, 80; temperature extremes, 85, 98; winter, xi, 52, 56–57, 97, 107

clothing, 25, 77, 94–95, 111

costs: of cows, 49; of farms, 47; of flour, 45; of land, 5, 6, 15, 45, 90, 108, 109; of oats, 18; of oxen, 49; of travel, 13, 15, 18, 35, 42, 43

crime, 110, 141–147. *See also* violence

cultural identities: Dutch, 30–34; German, xii, 87–88, 102–103, 107, 109–110; Norwegian, xii, 91, 95–99, 113–117; Swiss, 41–44; Wisconsin character, 157–163. *See also* American character

deaths: on frontier, 51, 62, 81, 82; at sea, 36, 37–38

diary entries: on anti-slavery movement, 127–131; on travels, 16–24, 30–39, 41–44

Dickens, Charles: *American Notes for General Circulation*, 143; *The Pickwick Papers*, 144, *145*

Diederichs, Johann Frederick, 44–48, 106–108

diet: on frontier, xii, 17, 19, 41–42, 44, 46–47, 75, 89, 112; at sea, 28–29, 30, 32, 33, 35, 37

diseases. *See* illnesses

divorce, petition for, 78–79

Dixon, Rev., 129–131

doctors, 12, 57–58, 60–61

dog trains, 73–75

Doty, James Duane, 152, 154

Drammen, 83, 114

Drummond, Rev., 62

Duerst, Mathias, 34–39, 41–44

Dutch immigrants, 26, 30–34

dysentery, 36

economic opportunities: farming, 8, 9–10, 45–46, 47, 90; generally, 101–103; schoolteachers, 68–69, 72, 118–120; tradespeople, 10, 12, 47

education. *See* schools and schoolteachers

Eggleston, Henry Seymour, x, 12–16

elections, 151–152

Fair Play, 129–131

farming and farmland: buying, 47, 103, 105–106; children's role, 9, 90; crops grown, 6, 45, 107–109; cultivating, 105–106; description of, 107–109; economic opportunities of, 8, 9–10, 45–46, 47, 90; farm life, 46–47, 48, 111; soil, 6, 96–97; wheat farming, 14–15

Ficker, Christian Traugott: description of American justice and politics, 12, 150–152; description of climate, 52–53; description of economic opportunities, 8–10; directions to Wisconsin from New York, 39–41; on earning a living, 101–103, 105–106; and guidebook for German immigrants, x, 8–9

Fidder, I. P., 68, 69, 70

Field, Alexander P., 143, 147

fires, 54–55, 106, 152

food. *See* diet

Foote, Sarah, x, 16–21

Frank, August, 110–112

Frank, Veronica (née Kerler), 110–112

freedom, promise of, 9, 85–86, 88–90, 136–138, 161–163

French settlers, xiv, 3

Fromader, George Adam, xii, 89–91

Fugitive Slave Law of 1850, 134–139

About the Author

Michael E. Stevens is Wisconsin State Historian Emeritus and the author or editor of thirteen books and nearly thirty articles. He has won the Gambrinus Prize for *The Family Letters of Victor and Meta Berger* and the Association for Documentary Editing's Lyman Butterfield Award for career contributions in historical research, teaching, and documentary editing. Stevens earned his PhD in American history from UW–Madison. He was editor and director of publications for the South Carolina Department of Archives and History from 1978 to 1987, and he held various positions at the Wisconsin Historical Society from 1987 to 2013, including state historian, state historic preservation officer, and division administrator.